Book of Hours

Book of Hours

Meditations
for the Heart after God

Jason David Eubanks, MD

DAWN TREADER

With love, to my heart's passion:
Jesus Christ,
my Lord and Savior.

...religious things have to do with a softly murmured soliloquy with oneself.

—Søren Kierkegaard

Books by Jason David Eubanks, MD

Twelve Stones: Apologetics for an Age of Relativism

Gentlest of Ways

More of Him, Less of Me:
A Doctor's Devotional for Spiritual Health

For the Joy of Obeying

Rotations: A Medical Student's Clinical Experience

Contents

Preface

The lasting characteristic of a spiritual man is the ability to understand correctly the meaning of the Lord Jesus Christ in his life, and the ability to explain the purposes of God to others. The overruling passion of his life is Jesus Christ. Whenever you see this quality in a person, you get the feeling that he is truly a man after God's own heart.

—Oswald Chambers, *My Utmost for His Highest*

What does it mean to be a man or woman "after God's own heart"? The very question almost seems presumptuous. For it implies the heart of God can be known, or at least conceptualized well enough to be pursued and obtained. But can man fathom the unfathomable? Can he grasp the ineffable?

King David was a man the prophet Samuel described as "a man after God's own heart"(1 Sam 13:14). Why? By way of context, Samuel's rebuke of King Saul gives us a clue. For when Saul failed to obey the Lord's command, Samuel tells us: a heart after God is marked by obedience. But in the years to come, David would soon prove just as disobedient as Saul. Indeed, David's sins are memorable. So a heart after God must mean more: humility, reverence, faithfulness, integrity, devotion, contrition, repentance, trust, perseverance, and above all else, love. It must mean a man whose passion is Jesus Christ.

David's psalms demonstrate this passion as they teach us what a heart after God looks like. And it is no mistake these nuanced lessons come in the language of poetry. For as Jewish theologian, Abraham Joshua Heschel, recognizes:

> To intercept the allusions that are submerged in perceptibilities, the interstitial values that never rise to the surface, the indefinable dimension of all existence, is the venture of true poetry. This is why poetry is to religion what analysis is to science, and it is certainly no

accident that the Bible was not written *more geometrico* but in the language of poets.[1]

In other words, spiritual matters don't fit into the explanations of neat equations. Rather, some creative consideration is often necessary to suss ultimate concerns. In this effort, poetry perhaps best helps us describe the indescribable. It puts some "flesh" on the ineffable. For as Russian poet, Marina Tsvetaeva, says, "What can we say about God? Nothing. What can we say *to* God? Everything. Poems to God are prayer."

David's psalms are a series of prayers that instruct us in the heart after God. No literature has moved my own heart after God more than these poems. I read them every morning and I pray them every night. And over the years, that indescribable something we call the "heart of God" becomes more and more knowable.

What follows in this *Book of Hours* is a series of prayers uttered by one heart after God's heart, to all those other hearts in pursuit. My prayer: In my seeking, may I help you in your finding.

—J.D. Eubanks, MD

---

[1] Abraham Joshua Heschel, *Man is Not Alone* (New York: Farrar, Straus, and Giroux, 1951), 37.

A thousand half-loves
must be forsaken to take
one whole heart home.
　　　　　　　—Rumi

Prelude

We live in a secular age. It is a time when the vaulted ceilings of churches and cathedrals have been given to the revelry of breweries and the Lycra legs of climbing gyms. The cup of Christ has, in places, been traded for a beer mug. Our nation's Puritan beginnings have devolved into moral relativism and absolute subjectivism. And even in those religious pockets where devotion remains, the congregant's "Sunday best" has often—for better or worse?—followed the cultural slide into casualness.

The "sacred" is being pushed to extinction. In this hunt, those special spaces that elevate the spirit by simply standing in them are disappearing. The mystical and divine beauty exemplified in chapels like Paris' Sainte-Chapelle has steadily been replaced with the functional utility of dressed-down "sanctuaries": Houses of worship or sterile stadiums? The holy relics that once filled cathedral apses have been tucked away into the dimly lit recesses of museums. In the midst of this vanishing act, awe and wonder for the ineffable have become increasingly rare.

But I still hunger for the "sacred." For somewhere between the lurid profanity of contemporary culture and the stark minimalism of some evangelical churches, some part of me longs—dare I say still needs—to *see* the cross, illuminated and lifted up. How to satisfy this craving?

On a rainy, Saturday afternoon in Cleveland, I head not to church, but to the Museum of Art. There, in the curated reverence of the Gothic period, I happen upon a book of hours for the late Queen Isabella of Spain (c. 1500 AD). One cannot help noticing the brilliantly ornate pages of this ancient devotional. A team of scribes and artists painstakingly composed and decorated this book for a pious queen. In my wonderment, I smile to think the devotions these vellum pages once inspired helped to launch the ships of Columbus. By the outworking of providential hands, the ground on which I now stand, in some sense, comes right back to this golden filigree.

1

It reminds me: what happens in our quiet moments moves out into the world. Sometimes, a whole new world.

I stand in that New World—a man, in blue jeans and well-worn Asics, peering into the privates pages of a devout queen. And in this New World, best-selling books look nothing like this exquisite Spanish relic. In the Late Middle Ages, however, a book of hours *was* the "best-seller" equivalent. It was an illuminated manuscript that served as a Christian devotional. At the peak of popularity, one in every four households owned such a book.

These books of hours ministered to those souls still living in what philosopher Charles Taylor dubs, "an enchanted world." That is, a world where the sacred still had a place in the everyday. And in this world, a book of hours commonly contained prayers and passages from the Gospels and the Psalms intended to direct the layperson's heart and mind toward God.

One of the many components of a typical book of hours included the seven penitential psalms (6, 32, 38, 51, 102, 130, 143). These psalms express sorrow over sin. Their inclusion in any book of hours was meant to help incline a supplicant's heart toward God in a prayerful remorse over inner iniquity. For as the Lord says through His prophet Joel, "Rend your heart…"(Joel 2:13). The penitential psalms aim to do just that.

The reflective and confessional focus of these psalms also guides the pages that follow. For like many of its Gothic predecessors, this *Book of Hours* incorporates the seven penitential psalms as a starting point for personal devotion. But moving out from these psalms, the meditations that expand from each scriptural passage seek to fulfill the *personal* essence of Joel's exhortation—to cleave the heart after God to God.

What results from this effort is, in a sense, a book of psalms within the Psalms. This intentional embedding does not attempt to alter, or substitute for, the divinely inspired Word. Rather, it aims to honor the Psalms with new life. For as Taylor points out:

> In relation of the literary cannon, the idea is that great poetry, in order to resonate again, needs a new context; otherwise put, it needs a range of contemporary voices, which can serve as its interlocutors, with which it can resonate.[2]

This *Book of Hours* attempts to "resonate" and amplify the ancient voice of the Psalms. For as the writer of Hebrews reminds us, "the Word of God is living and active…"(4:12). All that lives, of course, in some way moves.

---

[2] Charles Taylor, *A Secular Age* (Cambridge, MA: The Belknap Press, 2007), 759.

God's Word is no exception. It moves into hearts. And when it does, it changes them.

The following work chronicles the changes in my own heart, much as the Psalms do for David. My hope is that the meditations contained in this collection will help catalyze ongoing transformation in all those other hearts seeking after God. For while the journey of faith is a universal calling, it is not genuine until it moves from the universal to the personal. As poet Rainer Maria Rilke says, "...even the most visible happiness can't reveal itself to us until we transform it, within."[3] This book aims to help unveil the path to Heaven's happiness by demonstrating the gritty work of one man's inner transformation.

But as any disciple will tell you, the work of transformation is not only gritty, but also messy. It is an imperfect work that stumbles along. Yet it relentlessly keeps going: pursuing and pushing forward toward the perfection calling its name (Php 3:12-14).

Any written record of this journey must perforce be filled with a courageous candidness, part of what philosopher Paul Tillich might include in "the courage to be." For that is what I perhaps love most about the Psalms—particularly those penned by David: their plucky honesty of existence. Their heartfelt candor makes them real. And this "realness" proves them incredibly credible.

The meditations in this *Book of Hours* seek to exhibit this same candid vulnerability. They believe, even as they doubt. They cry out, even as they listen. They seek to obey, even as they long to run away. They love, even as they gently rebuff. For beating hearts are couplets of contraries. And the beating heart behind these meditations is no exception.

The Blueprint

In keeping with historic precedent, the seven penitential psalms anchor this *Book of Hours*. These seven psalms have then been divided into seventy-seven meditations. Of course, this numeric division is not without intent. For in a book devoted to penitential reflections and cries for forgiveness, the words between Jesus and Peter loom large:

---

[3] Rainer Maria Rilke, "Seventh Elegy" in *Duino Elegies & The Sonnets to Orpheus* (New York: Vintage International, 2009), 43.

3

Then Peter came to Jesus and asked, "Lord, how many times shall I forgive my brother when he sins against me? Up to seven times?" Jesus answered, "I tell you, not seven times, but seventy-seven times"(Mt 18:21-22).

Forgiveness, as Jesus reminds Peter, is not a "one-off." For whether it is God who chooses to forgive us, or we who must choose to forgive others, the call of forgiveness comes incessantly. The seventy-seven meditations that follow aim to solidify this principle.

Each individual meditation is then followed by readings from both the Old and New Testaments. These passages intend to illustrate and reinforce the concepts emerging from the preceding meditation. The reader who desires to most fully appreciate the emotive force behind the individual meditation, will be well-served by reading and reflecting on both these scriptures.

To further guide and aid this reflection, three questions then follow each set of readings. These questions intend to stimulate an introspective reflection and foster a prayerful spirit. Often, perspectives from outside voices are also included to more fully develop the thematic thrust of each meditation. For the interested reader, these references are then supplied for further exploration and personal edification. Among these references, each meditation is also linked with a specific devotional reading(s) from *More of Him, Less of Me: A Doctor's Devotional for Spiritual Health*. Readers may find this reference an instructive companion to the devotion time.

Ultimately, within the framework of this multi-tiered format, the meditations that follow strive to encourage, equip, and empower the heart after God to maintain its relentless pursuit of God. For as A.W. Tozer reminds us:

> God wants us to long for Him with the longing that will become lovesickness, that will become a wound to our spirits, to keep us always moving toward Him, always finding and always seeking, always having and always desiring.[4]

May this *Book of Hours* help inspire a lovesickness in your heart that finds you moving toward Christ, always seeking and always finding.

---

[4] A.W. Tozer, *Man—The Dwelling Place of God* (Public Domain).

The Hours

I.

Psalm 6

For the director of music. With stringed
instruments. According to *sheminith*. A psalm
of David.

O Lord, do not rebuke me in your anger
   or discipline me in your wrath.
Be merciful to me, Lord, for I am faint;
   O Lord, heal me, for my bones are in agony.
My soul is in anguish.
   How long, O Lord, how long?
Turn, O Lord, and deliver me;
   save me because of your unfailing love.
No one remembers you when he is dead.
   Who praises you from the grave?
I am worn out from groaning;
   all night long I flood my bed with weeping
   and drench my couch with tears.
My eyes grow weak with sorrow;
   they fail because of all my foes.
Away from me, all you who do evil,
   for the Lord has heard my weeping.
The Lord has heard my cry for mercy;
   the Lord accepts my prayer.
All my enemies will be ashamed and dismayed;
   they will turn back in sudden disgrace.

The First Hour

Psalm 6:1—O Lord, do not rebuke me in your anger
or discipline me in your wrath.

Your rebuke, O Lord,
  is your mercy's reckoning with my rebellion—
    and the mutineer in me wants no part of it.
Hold me and comfort me, speak softly to me,
  but spare me your reproof.
For I am reminded of your power in reproach,
  the rebuke which shakes the pillars of the heavens—
    a reprimand that calms the wind and the waves.
At your stern word, Lord, sickness flees;
  even the demons listen and obey.
The devil's teeming minions know
  how your rage is shown to your foes—
    how you will one day come with holy fire.
In whirlwind chariots, you will unleash your fury;
  your merciless rebuke will lash out
    with unrelenting tongues of flame.
At your judgement, O Lord,
  many will be slain by the angels' swords.

      ~

No, my Lord, I want no part
  of this angry rebuke!
It is enough to merely consider
  the disappointment in your eyes,
    much less the correction of your hands.
Do not discipline me in your wrath;
  spare me the rod of your punition.
Remember your solemn promise
  to bring me back with deep compassion,
    to gather me in the arms of everlasting kindness.
Recall your oath to Zion,
  your pledge to the faithful servants of the Lord:
  "I have sworn not to be angry with you,
    never to rebuke you again."

      ~

9

Still, without the possibility of your storm, Lord,
   there would be no hope for rain.
And what growth comes of empty, azure skies,
   in a parched and desolate desert?
Your tempests remind me: You rebuke
   and discipline those you love.
So I desire not the silence of feigned affection,
   but the honest candor of your heart.
For in your constant correction, I find my identity—
   true son of a Father
      whose unfailing love desires my good.
You are the Father
   whose disciplining hands redeem pain
      in your efforts to make me holy.
In the gentleness of your loving reproof,
   I am trained toward perfection;
you lead me forward to a harvest
   of righteousness and peace.

                    ~

But no man dreams to be Job, O Lord.
   For who longs for his trials of desolation?
And yet, Job's afflictions did not come
   because he was the worst of men—
      No! He was the best!
He was your beloved, God,
      and his name
   was on the tip of your tongue.
For blessed is the man you correct, Lord;
   and though you sometimes wound,
      you also bind us up.
Though you sometimes ravish us,
   the Sun of your righteousness will rise
      with healing in its wings.
So let your rebuke and discipline
   bind me in the bundle
      of your unfailing love.
May I never forget who I am—
   beloved son of a Father
      who loves me enough to wound me.
And though the Lord of Hosts may slay me,
      one day I shall come forth as gold.

<u>Selected Readings for Further Study</u>

† Job 1:6-12

† Hebrews 12:1-13

<u>Questions for Reflection and Prayer:</u>

1. Rebuke is never pleasant. But as Puritan preacher, Thomas Brooks, reminds us, the open rebuke of God in our lives is better than the alternative: "God is most angry when He shows no anger. God keep me from this mercy; this kind of mercy is worse than all other kind of misery." Why is God's absence of rebuke more concerning than His rebuke? When was the last time you felt the rebuke of God? Did you feel the heat of His anger, the warmth of His love, or a little bit of both? Was this rebuke in response to a specific sin in your life?

2. Can you dare to believe your Father disciplines you for your good? Can you think of a time when God's discipline in your life taught you something invaluable about yourself? About Him?

3. G.K. Chesterton reminds us that Job was tormented by the devil "not because he was the worst of men, but because he was the best." What can we learn about God's fatherly love from Job's afflictions?

References
>   1 Sam 25:29; Job 1:6-12; 5:17-18; 23:10; 26:11; Ps 119:2; Pr 13:24; 27:5; Isa 66:14-16; 54:9; Jer 23:19; Mal 4:2; Mt 17:18; Mk 4:39; 8:33; Lk 4:39; 2 Tim 3:16; 4:2; Heb 12:1-13; Rev 3:19

<u>Diving Deeper:</u>

1. J.D. Eubanks, MD, "God's Gold" in *More of Him, Less of Me* (Dawn Treader, LLC, 2018), 200.
2. Thomas Brooks, *Precious Remedies Against Satan's Devices* (Public Domain).
3. G.K. Chesterton, "The Book of Job" in *The Defense of Sanity* (San Francisco: Ignatius Press, 2011), 102.

Psalm 6:2—Be merciful to me, Lord, for I am faint;
O Lord, heal me, for my bones are in agony.

O Lord, faintness of heart
　　is the hard-earned
　　　　feeling of the faithful,
the weary legs beneath those fighters
　　who are fought out
　　and near to falling.
For no one follows your footsteps, Lord,
　　　without growing
　　weak at the knees;
and the true testament of commitment
　　is not the first strides of the race,
　　but the mid-marathon's exhaustion.
Perhaps we only wear out,
　　because our hope is not in you.
Maybe we only grow tired,
　　because we look for strength
　　　in all the wrong places.
But even the hope that renews our strength—
　　that mounts us on the wings of eagles
　　and causes us to run without weariness—
even this hope takes strength to hope,
　　　and sometimes the soul's matchbook
　　seems too wet to spark darkness into flame.
Will you fill up my empty tank, Lord?
　　Can you plant your seed of promise
　　　in the dustbowl of my soul?
For when I stand in the valley of dry bones,
　　　all I see is a skeletal sea
　　dressed in a mealy white.
And unless your Spirit comes down
　　and breathes His life into me—
unless He dresses my inner agony
　　in the sinews of Heaven—
I will never rise to the riches
　　waiting for the righteous.

Almighty God, you are both
  the Father I long to embrace
  and the Judge to whom I plead for mercy.
You are my Creator and my King,
    the God who has mercy
  on whom He will have mercy,
    and compassion
  on whom He will have compassion.
In this hour, I long for your mercy, Lord;
  the bones of my soul
  cry out for your compassion.
For even Moses sought your compassion;
    he became a man like me,
  who pleaded for the mercy of your Presence.
With fearful courage he said,
    "Teach me your ways
  so I may know you and find favor with you."
With boldness the prophet entreated you,
    "Now show me your glory!"
And in the gentle might of your mercy, O God,
  you passed all your goodness before him.
Now show me this glory, Lord!
  Hide me in a rocky cleft if you must,
    but let your goodness stride before me.
Then maybe the hem of your robe
  will touch my soul's fatigue,
    and the fainthearted will be full
  of the Fear of Heaven.
Then perhaps my sleeping spirit will rise,
  like Lazarus from the tomb
    and Dorcas from the bed.
And then maybe, just maybe,
    my pile of bones
  will push up from the grave
    to stand on their feet again...
if only you, Almighty God,
    bid the four winds breathe the breath
  of your Presence into my death.
For in this valley of dry bones,
  O Sovereign Lord, only you know
    how to make men from the Man
    who made hope, hope.
Make this Man in me!

<u>Selected Readings for Further Study</u>

† Exodus 33:12-23

† Acts 9:36-42

<u>Questions for Reflection and Prayer:</u>

1. Puritan preacher, Thomas Goodwin, says punishment is God's "strange work, but mercy pleases Him; He is the 'Father of mercies,' He begets them naturally." As Goodwin notes, God gives mercy freely because it is in His nature. Can you list the mercies of God in your life this very day? When was the last time you received mercy from someone you love? From someone who persecuted you?

2. Do you believe, as Goodwin points out, "Your misery can never exceed His [God's] mercy"? How does this truth help free us from the shackles of sin and suffering? Can you believe God is able to make you soar on the wings of an eagle?

3. In his opus on the Russian penal system under Stalin, *The Gulag Archipelago*, Nobel Laureate Aleksandr Solzhenitsyn says, "A human being is all hope and impatience." The problem, of course, is hope and impatience are oil and water: they don't mix. For hope without patience only results in a frustrated discontent, prone to anxiety, resignation and despair. Have you ever been so thin on patience that your hope felt dead? How did you get there? What is the antidote to this problem?

References
> Ex 33:19; Dt 32:39; 2 Ki 20:5; Ne 9:31; Job 9:15; Isa 53:5; 55:6-7; 63:9; Jer 13:14; 17:14; 21:7; 30:17; 33:6; Eze 37:1-15; Hos 6:6; 14:4; Mic 6:8; Mt 5:7; Lk 1:50; 4:40; 7:7; 18:42; Jn 11:38-44; Acts 9:36-42; Ro 9:16; 12:1; Eph 2:4; Jas 2:13; 1 Pe 1:3

<u>Diving Deeper:</u>

1. J.D. Eubanks, MD, "Mercy Triumphs" in *More of Him, Less of Me* (Dawn Treader, LLC, 2018), 33.
2. Thomas Goodwin, *The Heart of Christ* (King Solomon, 2020), 45, 69.
3. Aleksandr Solzhenitsyn, *The Gulag Archipelago* (New York: Harper & Row, 1974). 574.

The Third Hour

Psalm 6:3—My soul is in anguish.
How long, O Lord, how long?

How long, O Lord, how long?

How long before Heaven's stairs
come tumbling down
beneath the glorious weight of you?
How long before Heaven's tardy kiss
heals your heavy hearts?
Anguish lives there,
on the narrow path
between pain and privation—
in the lonely valley,
where anger loses it voice
and sorrow knows no surcease.
Anguish walks in a crowd
oblivious to its bleeding,
while it longs for a strangled word
with a world that has no time.
But because anguish is love's offspring,
its roots reach back to you, Lord.
The deeper it dives,
the higher it might hope to fly;
and the force of its wave
draws from the depth of affection—
only you know how....
it feels to be the weeping woman
kneeling at your altar,
drunk,
not on wine, but sorrow
sick with longing for new life.
Only you can guess
at the pain of the prophet's vision
as he cries out:
"Oh, my anguish, my anguish!
I writhe in pain.
Oh the agony of my heart!
My heart pounds within me;
I cannot keep silent."

15

Only you know, Lord,
  because only your anguish
    sweat drops of blood.
You entered in, not to explain,
    but to experience;
you bared your flesh,
  not to simply commiserate,
    but to mediate.
So Sodom may sing into the night
  that will never see the dawn,
but your servant will greet the morning
  with a grief that gives way to joy.
Like a mother giving birth,
    the labor pains will break upon
  a joy no one can steal.
And the silence that long rebuffs suffering,
      will at last
  burst into songs of deliverance.
But until anguish melts into this morning,
    faith must be the footbridge
  that links our brokenness to you, Lord.[5]
And no one—but you, God—knows
  if the ropes will hold, until
    one plank at a time,
  he steps toward you.
But you listen as we dare, Lord;
  you supply as we need.
In a world that will not hear,
    you, Father, are all ear
  for the suffering that peels
    the rind off
  the sweetness of your love.
And when the husk is finally gone,
    I will sink my teeth
  into the only flesh that can satisfy
    the hunger anguish has left.
For if I open my mouth wide,
  you promise to fill it
    with the fruit
  that finally makes sense
    of this ceaseless suffering.

---

[5] Nicholas Wolterstorff, *Lament for a Son* (Grand Rapids, MI: W.B. Eerdman's, 1987), 76.

Selected Readings for Further Study

† Jeremiah 4:5-22

† John 16:17-28

Questions for Reflection and Prayer:

1. Anton Chekhov's short story, "Anguish," describes a cab driver burdened with a sorrow he longs to share with his passengers who are all too busy to notice his suffering. As Chekhov says, "But the crowds rush by, noticing neither him nor his anguish....It [anguish] has managed to fit itself into such an insignificant shell that it is invisible in broad daylight...." Have you felt the loneliness of anguish? Have you considered God may be in the indifferent crowd, longing to listen to you?

2. It is good and right to feel anguish in our hearts for the godlessness of the world around us. But what do we learn from the sulfurous rains that destroyed Sodom, and the Babylonian army that razed Jerusalem? Is there a limit to God's patience with perversity? How does this reality inform our anguish? How does a knowledge of what is yet to come inform our lives in the present?

3. Have you found in Christ the answer to your soul's grief? Can grief itself be God's messenger in our lives? Søren Kierkegaard says, "And when God wishes to bind a human being to Him in earnest, He summons one of His most faithful servants, His truest messenger, Grief, and tells him: Hurry after him, overtake him, and don't budge from his side." Have you allowed your grief to cleave you to Christ?

References
Dt 6:5; 1 Sam 1:15-16; Job 10:1; Ps 42:1-2; 81:10; 119:28, 81; Isa 38:15-17; Jer 4:5-22; Mt 16:26; Lk 22:44; Jn 12:27; 16:21; 2 Cor 2:4; Heb 6:19; 2 Pe 2:18

Diving Deeper:

1. J.D. Eubanks, MD, "Turned to Joy" in *More of Him, Less of Me* (Dawn Treader, LLC, 2018), 284.
2. Anton Chekhov, "Anguish" in *Fifty-two Stories* (New York: Vintage Classics, 2021), 52.
3. Søren Kierkegaard, *The Diary of Søren Kierkegaard* (New York: Citadel Press, 1988), 20.

17

The Fourth Hour

Psalm 6:4—Turn, O Lord, and deliver me;
save me because of your unfailing love.

Turning, turning, all
  is always turning—
the world on its axis,
    fortune on its wheel,
      the heart on its fickle affections.
In this hour I confess, Lord,
  I too have turned away;
for a time, I gave my back to you,
  not my face.
Like your unfaithful people,
   my heart courted other gods—
     I was chief among them.
I attempted to turn things
  upside down,
    as if the Potter were the clay,
  and clay the Potter.
In the depth of my sorrow,
  I even asked you to turn away;
with Job, I sought a moment's reprieve
  to wallow in my self-pity.
     ~

Forgive me, Lord, for my sin,
  and the faith that fails
    more than it succeeds.
For I have turned to the right and left;
  I have neglected your path.
And I know, that when aroused,
   your anger won't turn from my rebellion,
    until it accomplishes your heart's purposes.
Bracing this bleak forecast,
  I will speak of your promises.
For have you not declared,
  "Turn to me and be saved"?
Have you not spoken
  through unclean lips, touched:

"Let the wicked forsake his way
    and the evil man his thoughts.
Let him turn to the Lord,
    and He will have mercy on him"?

~

In this hope, I turn my face to you, God.
    I seek you while you may be found.
Bring me back with deep compassion;
    turn my mourning into gladness.
Give me tomorrow's comfort and joy,
    instead of today's sickness and sorrow.
Send me the strong arms
    of your divine consolation.
And though you refine me
    in the furnace of affliction,
        sustain me with your tender affection.
For the heart of man desires unfailing love;
    and Love designed desire
        to bring the heart home.
But where can we find it,
    this love that never fails?
For men may claim unwavering loyalty;
    women may promise unceasing affection.
    But who has discovered a faithful heart?
Only the Lord's lovingkindness is limitless;
    only the Father can back the promise
to never leave me or forsake me.
For you have declared, Lord,
    that though the mountains be shaken
        and the hills removed,
your unfailing love will not waver,
    or your covenant of peace be revoked.
Though the world crumbles and scatters,
    your unflagging affection will never veer.
For your love, Lord, is my salvation:
    the point of beginning, ending,
        and turning—
and the only vantage to view
    the unfathomable expanse
        of this life and the next.
Your love, O Lord, is all
    that will ever be tried and true.

19

Selected Readings for Further Study

† Jeremiah 32:30-35; Isaiah 54:6-10

† Matthew 24:1-35

Questions for Reflection and Prayer:

1. Have you turned your back to God rather than your face? Or, are you still blaming God for turning away from you? Are you seeking Him while He may be found?

2. Kierkegaard contends the love of God is "the only unshakable thing in life, the true Archimedean point." Elsewhere he goes on to say:

> The hidden life of love is in the most inward depths, unfathomable, and still has an unfathomable relationship with the whole of existence. As the quiet lake is fed deep down by the flow of hidden springs, which no eye sees, so a human being's love is grounded, still more deeply, in God's love. If there were no spring at the bottom, if God were not love, then there would be neither a little lake nor a man's love.

Do you believe that God's love is the unfailing spring? Is it the Archimedean point of your life? Can you rest in the promises God's love has made? And if not, why?

3. How can the story of God's relentless affection for Israel be an encouragement to your weary heart? Can you see in God's love for Israel a God who keeps His promises?

References
Ex 32:12; Lev 19:4, 31; Nu 32:15; Dt 5:32; Job 10:20; Ps 32:10; 36:7; 62:12; Pr 19:22; 20:6; Isa 22:4; 29:16; 45:22; 54:7, 10; 55:7; Jer 17:13; 30:24; 31:13; 32:33; Mt 24:1-35

Diving Deeper:

1. J.D. Eubanks, MD, "God Amidst 'gods'" in *More of Him, Less of Me* (Dawn Treader, LLC, 2018), 216.
2. Søren Kierkegaard, *The Diary of Søren Kierkegaard* (New York: Citadel Press, 1988), 33.
3. Søren Kierkegaard, *Works of Love* (New York: HarperPerennial, 2009), 27.

The Fifth Hour

Psalm 6:5—No one remembers you [Lord] when he is dead.
Who praises you from the grave?

Who is Death to you, Lord,

but a warden of the needless night
  we have brought upon ourselves?
Dressed in his dark robe,
  wielding his scythe,
he was born of our disobedience.
He ranges the earth to exact his price,
  and round one of the fight
    always falls in his favor.
It is the only equality without election,
  and the only end without escape—
    save salvation.
For each man is his own grave,
  a tomb of his own making;
  and until he decides to die to himself,
    he cannot climb out.
He is buried alive in the death he bears,
    sealed in the soil
  of the sin he has chosen.
But his casket will not keep him
  from your coming judgement, Lord;
and the grave will soon spit him out,
  before the feet of Heaven's magistrate.
For all men will rise
  before the bell's tone of round two;
and though Death's blows
    may have stolen
  the memory of former things,
the books will be opened
  for history's retelling.
Whether a man sings or screams,
  depends upon whose side he has chosen.
Will he keep rising
  into the Light of the living,
or descend with the shrieking procession
  that follows the death of Death?

21

The one who believes in you, Lord,
  will live, even though he dies.
For the path of his life will lead upward,
  away from the grave's final descent.
When he rises from his sleep,
    you will say,
  "Take off his grave clothes
      and let him go."
But the one who rejects the Son
    will not see life,
  for the rod of Heaven remains on him.
With Death, he will be catapulted
  into the fiery lake;
he will long for the love of Lazarus,
    and the cool finger
  on his searing tongue.
But my tongue has been touched
  by Heaven's fire;
on this side of the grave,
  it will sing your praise, Lord.
For like the Son of Man,
  I will rise from the tomb.
The agony of death
  cannot hold me;
the chains of Sheol
  will not detain my soul.
For the Spirit's fire burns
  on the altar of my heart.
And when Death reaches for me,
    he will only singe his hands
  on Eternity's flame.
"Where, O Death, is your victory?
  Where, O Death, is your sting."
You are not the warden of my night,
    but the doorway from this dream
  into the unending light.
For my night has been turned
    into the immortal day;
and though the grave will grasp,
    I will walk through
  the walls of wailing—
      changed into the unchangeable.

<u>Selected Readings for Further Study</u>

† Psalm 49:13-20

† 1 Corinthians 15:20-57

<u>Questions for Reflection and Prayer:</u>

1. In a world that attempts to legislate equality, there is only one law that affects all men equally: Death. As the Stoic philosopher Seneca says, "Death is not an evil. What is it then? The one law mankind has that is free of all discrimination." When you consider the inevitability of death, how do you feel? Afraid, apprehensive, or filled with an anticipatory delight?

2. Another Stoic, Marcus Aurelius, encourages us to *welcome* death. He says, "Don't look down on death, but welcome it….Now you anticipate the child's emergence from its mother's womb, that's how you should await the hour when your soul will emerge from its compartment." How is the Christian specifically equipped to welcome death? Is death the end or the beginning—the life coming forth from the womb? For the Christian, will death be followed by a bodiless existence, or will our immortal souls be coupled with glorified bodies (1 Cor 15:42-44; Php 3:21)?

3. The Apostle Paul declares, "Christ has indeed been raised from the dead, the firstfruits of those who have fallen asleep"(1 Cor 15:20). When the last enemy— Death—is defeated by Christ, the perishable will be clothed with the imperishable and the mortal with immortality. If this is our promise, then Seneca is right: "death is so little to be feared that through its good offices nothing is to be feared." What shall you fear?

References
> Job 26:6; Ps 49:13-20; Pr 15:24; Hos 13:14; Amos 9:2; Lk 11:24; Jn 3:36; 11:25; 1 Cor 15:42-57; Php 3:21; Rev 20:14-15

<u>Diving Deeper:</u>

1. J.D. Eubanks, MD, "The Dying Gift" in *More of Him, Less of Me* (Dawn Treader, LLC, 2018), 144.
2. Seneca, *Letters from a Stoic* (Public Domain).
3. Marcus Aurelius, *Meditations* (Public Domain).

The Sixth Hour

Psalm 6:6—I am worn out from groaning;
all night long I flood my bed with weeping
and drench my couch with tears.

Heavenly Father, I know our groaning

needn't fall into grumbling,
and the soul that moans
need not stoop to gripe.
But the desert road
is rough on resilience,
and even the bravest of souls
might slip
from tears to tirades.
It is the caviling that kills us,
not the wailing;
it is the carping that condemns,
not the weeping.
For you are close to the brokenhearted;
and those who mourn
will be blessed.
And while every complaint drives a wedge
between earth and Heaven,
grief's wisdom grovels
its way to future greatness.
It bows at your feet, Lord,
to soak your toes in its sorrow;
with long tresses,
grief wipes the tears
of its broken knowing
from the flesh of the One
who has always known.
O Lord, you came to gather the groaning,
those worn-out souls
whose sympathy for self
has finally reached land's end.
For self-pity is the sin that whines,
as it throws God down from His throne
before the delight of inner demons.

In its hurricane of complaints,
  pity feeds the swirling
    monster of its making,
  building strength
till resolution starves it out,
  or you, God, drive it
    into the desert to die.
But the heart that groans
  speaks the universe's voice,
    as it joins the guttural chorus of creation—
the meadows that mewl in the morning,
  and the wind that howls through the night;
the waves that exhale a crashing sigh,
  and the clouds that cry giant tears
    for the Kingdom's coming birth.
Broken spirits in a broken world,
  longing to be clothed
    with our heavenly dwelling.
For since Eden's gates closed,
  the earth has been drenched in tears.
And if it were not for your promise, Lord,
  the world would've remained a flood.
But as you once gathered the waters,
  you will one day gather the groaning.
For the dwelling of God
  will be with men,
and Heaven will be earth,
  and earth will be Heaven.
Lord, you will wipe every tear
  from the weary eyes,
and satisfy the groan
  of every hungry heart.
The paradigm of pain will vanish
  in the blinding newness of things;
and the flood of men's tears
  will finally recede
    over a leafing land,
where the mountains rise
  into the rainbow running from you—
    the King who comes on clouds
      to claim the called.

25

<u>Selected Readings for Further Study</u>

† Ezekiel 21:6-7; 24:15-27

† Luke 7:36-50

<u>Questions for Reflection and Prayer:</u>

1. God hates grumbling for at least two reasons: It stems from ingratitude and it displaces Him from the center of the heart. As a result, James says, "Don't grumble…or you will be judged. The Judge is standing at the door!"(Jas 5:9). Is your heart filled with the idolatrous ingratitude of grumbling?

2. Oswald Chambers speaks to the destructive nature of self-pity when he says:

> No sin is worse than the sin of self-pity, because it removes God from the throne of our lives, replacing Him with our own self-interests. It causes us to open our mouths only to complain, and we simply become spiritual sponges—always absorbing, never giving, and never being satisfied.

Have you allowed self-pity to remove God from the throne of your life? Has self-pity moved you from groaning to grumbling?

3. Twentieth century philosopher, Martin Buber, says, "Creation is not a hurdle on the road to God, it is the road itself." If so, when creation groans (Ro 8:22), how can it help lead our hearts home? Can you hear the groaning of creation? Does it resonate with a similar groaning in your spirit (Ro 8:23)?

References
> Ge 6-9; Nu 14:26-30; Ps 38:8; Pr 29:2; Isa 25:8; La 1:16; Eze 21:6-7; 24:15-27; Lk 7:38, 44; Ro 8:22-23; 2 Cor 5:2-4; Jas 5:9

<u>Diving Deeper:</u>

1. J.D. Eubanks, MD, "Grumbling" in *More of Him, Less of Me* (Dawn Treader, LLC, 2018), 339.
2. Oswald Chamber, *My Utmost for His Highest* (Grand Rapids, MI: Discovery House Publishers, 1992), May 16.
3. Martin Buber, *Between Man and Man* (Victoria, Canada: Must Have Books, 2021), 52.

The Seventh Hour

Psalm 6:7—My eyes grow weak with sorrow;
they fail because of all my foes.

W hy, O Lord, have you thrown me
  up against the wall
    where the fighting is fiercest,
where the arrows rain down
  to raze me in another man's rage?
Is faithfulness a fool's errand
    crowned only with self-sacrifice,
  for a king
who is, who knows where,
  doing who knows what?
Don't tell me
  he's striding his parapets,
  eyeing the only lamb I have.
Spare me the truth
  I'm fighting his war,
  while he plots against me.
True, I've signed on to this campaign
  with full consent.
I've pledged my loyalty
  to his royalty.
I've given my heart and soul
  to fight what I thought
  was the good fight.
But why would Heaven allow
    the letter that leaves me
on the frontline, all alone?
Why send word to withdraw
  my battle-hardened brothers—
abandoned and exposed?
What have I done
  to deserve desertion?
Perhaps fidelity only earns affliction,
    and your purposes, Lord, work best
  through the drenched
    sword's tip.

27

For behind his fortifications,
  the enemy is a towering
    wall of water,
crashing down
  before an ocean of endless waves—
  but is he my enemy or yours?
At times, this fight seems full
  of flesh and blood;
at times the battle ranks
  appear filled with so much more.
Am I grappling with giants,
  or wrestling with wraiths?
My eyes grow weak with sorrow;
  they fail because of all my foes.
My eyes fail, looking for your promise;
  I say, "When will you comfort me?"
But even if your plan, Lord,
  leaves my body on the field,
    grant me one last wish:
Give me the sight to see
  you are still with me.
Open my eyes to espy
  the hills full of your horses,
    their chariots of fire in tow.
Show me the legions
  of your faithfulness;
peel the scales from my vision
  to unveil your hidden glory.
Help me to see in this battle,
  light and momentary troubles,
achieving for me an eternal glory
  that far outweighs them all.
Fix my eyes, not on what is seen,
  but on what is unseen—
    the victory dance of Heaven.
For though the heart of man
    plans his ways,
  the Lord determines his steps.
And even if I fall before this wall,
    one day
  Love will finally have had its way,
as I stand next to the Lamb
  no mortal king can steal from me.

Selected Readings for Further Study

† 2 Samuel 11

† 2 Corinthians 4:16-18

Questions for Reflection and Prayer:

1. Can you think of a time—maybe it is now?—when challenges crashed into your life with the almost rhythmic succession of the ocean's waves? How did [is] God sustain[ing] you in that time?

2. Are you facing constant enemies because you are fighting the good fight? Or, are your battles the result of your own disobedience? Could your difficulties be the result of Moses' prophetic warning to the wayward heart (Dt 28:28-67)?

3. Uriah's story is a troubling one. He appears to be the victim of a larger narrative. But C.S. Lewis reminds us of the following:

> The world is a dance in which good, descending from God, is disturbed by evil arising from the creatures, and the resulting conflict is resolved by God's own assumption of the suffering nature which evil produces. The doctrine of the free Fall asserts that evil which thus makes the fuel or raw material for the second and more complex kind of good is not God's contribution but man's.

As Lewis notes, even the kind of evil committed against Uriah can be redeemed by God into a "more complex kind of good." Can you see how God has redeemed the evil against Uriah in your own life? How has his contribution to David's development helped to change your heart?

References
     Dt 28:28-67; 34:7; 2 Sa 11; Ki 6:17; Job 17:7; Ps 31:9; Ps 119:82, 123;
     Pr 16:9; Isa 43:8; La 2:11, 5:17; Mt 6:22-23; Acts 9:18; 2 Cor 4:16-18

Diving Deeper:

1. J.D. Eubanks, MD, "Never Outnumbered" in *More of Him, Less of Me* (Dawn Treader, LLC, 2018), 268.
2. C.S. Lewis, *The Problem of Pain* (New York: HarperCollins, 1996), 80.

The Eighth Hour

Psalm 6:8-9—Away from me, all you who do evil,
for the Lord has heard my weeping.
The Lord has heard my cry for mercy;
the Lord accepts my prayer.

Father, I know you hear my prayers,
  just as Christ's before me.
And yet, even in His confidence,
  my Savior suffered in Gethsemane.
For though you catch our cries,
  do our cries always cry out
    for your will?
Do you always answer our prayers
  in their nascent imaginings,
    in the instance of our insistence?
Or must we, like the submitted Son,
    first cry out,
  "Not my will, but yours be done"?
Yet even reverent submission
    is no guarantee
  the cross will not come.
And the head that bows
    may still weep tears of blood,
  betrayed by a kiss.
Why should we be spared
  the sorrow of your Son?
I know better than to join Jabez
  in his insular prayer.
For how will I identify
  with the Man of Sorrows
    in a wishful life
  free of pain and suffering?
And if there is no weeping,
    then there is no living,
  and comfort has nowhere to come.
If there is no struggle,
  your mercy may not move.

30

But you desire mercy, Lord,
   and your compassion holds hands
      with your unfailing love.
And though my sins
      threaten to sink me,
   your grace reaches for the rescue.
In your patience with the drowning,
      you have made known
   to the objects of your mercy
      the riches of your glory.
So with the seer I pray,
   "Lord, I have heard of your fame;
      I stand in awe of your deeds, O Lord.
   Renew them in our day,
      in our time make them known;
      in wrath remember mercy."
Send us the angel of your Presence, Lord;
   in your love and mercy redeem us;
      lift us up and carry us.
Then my soul will rest content
   to be the Canaanite cur
      beneath the table,
   eating the scraps of your banquet.
For better is one day in your house,
   than a thousand elsewhere;
better to be the cherished mutt
   at the feet of Majesty,
than the empurpled king
  raging against his fading fantasy.
For the kings of this world
   will come to nothing;
but the small, broken voice
   will hook Heaven's ear.
And if the believer only hangs on
   to the bending line he has cast,
what he lands
   will break the nets of hope—
      for even the highest heavens
      cannot contain Him.

Selected Readings for Further Study

† 1 Chronides 4:9-10

† Matthew 15:21-28

Questions for Reflection and Prayer:

1. When it comes to finding the will of God for our lives, South African pastor, Andrew Murray, speaks to our impatient insistence when he says:

> How often we ask: "How can a person know the will of God?" And people want, when they are in perplexity, to pray very earnestly that God should answer them at once. But God can only reveal His will to a heart that is humble and tender and empty. God can only reveal His will in perplexities and special difficulties to a heart that has learned to obey and honor Him in little things and in daily life.

If God has not yet answered your prayer, is it because your heart is not "humble and tender and empty"? Are you obeying and honoring Him in the "little things"?

2. How can we not, like Jabez, wish for a life free from pain and suffering? But even if God were to grant us such a wish, at what cost would it come? Would it be worth it? Do you think Jesus would have considered making that request of our Father?

3. What can we learn from the Canaanite woman who debases herself before Jesus (Mt 15: 21-28)? She is rewarded by Christ. Why? Are you willing to be the "dog" beneath God's table?

References
1 Ki 8: 27; 1 Ch 4:9-10; Isa 55:7; 63:9; Hos 6:6; Hab 3:2; Mt 15: 21-28; Ro 9: 22-23; 1 Tim 1:16

Diving Deeper:

1. J.D. Eubanks, MD, "The Prayer of Jabez" in *More of Him, Less of Me* (Dawn Treader, LLC, 2018), 362.
2. Andrew Murray, *Absolute Surrender* (Public Domain).

The Ninth Hour

Psalm 6:10—All my enemies will be ashamed and dismayed;
they will turn back in sudden disgrace.

Shameless, God,

    our world is a brazen beauty
stretched out beside countless shrines.
She calls evil good and good evil,
  even as she puts darkness for light
  and light for darkness.
With willful disdain,
  she prostitutes herself
  before a host of idols;
bare-breasted and bold,
  now telling all her untolds
    with pride, not apology.
Far from the naked perfection
  of your Garden, O Lord,
  and the shamelessness of essence—
when in the precious ignorance of innocence,[6]
  we walked before you
    in an unencumbered purity.
Now is the critical contempt
  of conscious spurning,
the iron-clad obstinacy
  of hearts that refuse to bow.
These plans were not your hopes, Lord,
    but the upshot of an alliance
forged in a common resistance
    only your love can rectify.
Yet have the rebels forgotten, God,
  what treaties with darkness bring?
Can they not see the flimsy arm of Pharaoh,
  who brings neither help, nor advantage,
    but shame and disgrace?

---

[6] Søren Kierkegaard, "Dread and Freedom" in *Existentialism From Dostoevsky to Sartre*, ed. Walter Kaufmann (New York: Plume, 1975), 101.

Their wickedness is a squall that blinds them;
   in their foolishness they trust in flesh,
   even as they throw out shame.
But what good is a world without shame,
    if it darkens our view
   of the road of repentance?
For though chagrin comes,
   the righteous are not imprisoned;
and without the suffering of shame,
   how will we ever find Heaven's righteousness?
The only shame is to have no shame;
   and in a shameless world,
    there is no place for righteousness.
But without righteousness,
    how will we stand before you?
Holy Spirit, in this hour I pray,
   lead us to Heaven's sense of shame.
In an adulterous age,
  set our faces like flint.
For you have promised the righteous
   an everlasting salvation.
Have you not declared for us
    a double portion,
   instead of everlasting ignominy?
The one who trusts in you, God,
   will receive your inheritance,
   the eternal joy of your Presence.
But to the shameless you will show
   unending shame,
as the truth they denied unveils
   separation, disgrace, and eternal dismay.
For you, God, cannot be mocked;
   and a man reaps what he sows.
The one who sows in shamelessness,
    will reap the howling
   of a bitter wind.
But as for me, I embrace the shame
   that draws me to you, Lord;
for in a fallen world,
   it is a rod gently used
    to make me more like you.

Selected Readings for Further Study

† Isaiah 30:1-5; 61:7-11

† Romans 9:30-33

Questions for Reflection and Prayer:

1. Is there a place for shame in our spiritual lives? The contemporary culture teaches shame as a negative emotion? Is it always? C.S. Lewis points out the following:

> We are told to "get things out into the open," not for the sake of self-humiliation, but on the grounds that these "things" are very natural and we need not be ashamed of them. But unless Christianity is wholly false, the perception of ourselves which we have in moments of shame must be the only true one; and even Pagan society has usually recognized "shamelessness" as the nadir of the soul. In trying to extirpate shame we have broken down one of the ramparts of the human spirit, madly exulting in the work as the Trojans exulted when they broke their walls and pulled the Horse into Troy.

When we push for a "shameless" culture, are we advocating for a Christian one?

2. When poet Wendell Berry says, "Praise ignorance, for what a man / has not yet encountered he has not yet destroyed," he echoes Kierkegaard's Edenic "ignorance of innocence." How does Eden's story link ignorance and shame (Genesis 3)?

3. Why should the redeemed have no fear of shame? And why should the shameless—those who willfully reject God—live in mortal fear of shame?

References
> Ge 2:25; Pr 18:3; Isa 5:20; 30:1-5; 44:9; 45:17; 50:7; 54:4; 61:7; Jer 3:3; 6:15; Zep 3:5; Ro 9:33; Gal 6:7-8

Diving Deeper:

1. J.D. Eubanks, MD, "The Weeping Necessity" in *More of Him, Less of Me* (Dawn Treader, LLC, 2018), 6.
2. J.D. Eubanks, MD, "Shame: The Voice of the Godly Conscience" in *For the Joy of Obeying* (Dawn Treader, LLC, 2019), 34-41.
3. C.S. Lewis, *The Problem of Pain* (New York: HarperCollins, 1996), 50.
4. Wendell Berry, "Manifesto: The Mad Farmer Liberation Front."

II.

Psalm 32

Of David. A *maskil*.

Blessed is he
  whose transgressions are forgiven,
  whose sins are covered.
Blessed is the man
  whose sin the Lord does not count
    against him
  and in whose spirit is no deceit.
When I kept silent,
  my bones wasted away
  through my groaning all day long.
For day and night
  your hand was heavy upon me;
my strength was sapped
  as in the heat of summer.
Then I acknowledged my sin to you
  and did not cover up my iniquity.
I said, "I will confess
  my transgressions to the Lord"—
and you forgave
  the guilt of my sin.
Therefore let everyone who is godly
  pray to you while you may be found;
surely when the mighty waters rise,
  they will not reach him.
You are my hiding place;
  you will protect me from trouble
  and surround me with songs of deliverance.

I will instruct you and teach you
  in the way you should go;
  I will counsel you and watch over you.
Do not be like the horse or the mule,
  which have no understanding
but must be controlled by bit and bridle
  or they will not come to you.
Many are the woes of the wicked,
  but the Lord's unfailing love
  surrounds the man who trusts in Him.
Rejoice in the Lord and be glad, you righteous;
  sing all you who are upright in heart!

The Tenth Hour

Psalm 32: 1-2—Blessed is he whose transgressions are forgiven,
whose sins are covered.
Blessed is the man
whose sin the Lord does not
count against him,
and in whose spirit is no deceit.

The cross cries: "Father, forgive them,

for they know not what they do!"
But is this always true, Lord?
For your enemy says, "God is dead,"
and we have killed him, you and I—
the blood is on our hands.
We have screamed,
"Crucify him, crucify him!"
Before the prevaricating Pilate,
we have indicted ourselves—
"Let his blood be on us."
We have spit on your face, Lord,
cursed your Holy Name,
and crowned you with twisted thorns.
We have dared to live dangerously,
and to celebrate our deed—
to make ourselves gods,
simply to seem worthy of it.
But I wonder, O Lord,
if it hasn't made you laugh so hard
that you cry.
For what pack of fools
would imagine Heaven could be owned
and slaughtered like a lamb,
unless the Lamb lay down
of its own accord?
"Who will wipe this blood off us?
What water will cleanse us?
What sacred rites shall we invent
to acquit ourselves?
How will the murderers of all murderers,
comfort the consciences

39

of all those convicted killers?"
The greatness of the deed doesn't dwell
  in the murderous shout from the crowd,
    but the soft words from the cross.
It is not, "God is dead" and "God remains dead,"
  but, "It is finished" and "He is risen."
Fortunate is the man
  whose recognition reins in
  his reckless reasoning.
He is the rebel who might be redeemed;
  he is the dead man who might be raised.
His is the chasm that might be crossed;
  his is the sickness that might be healed.
For there is a grace that greets the bow,
  and a mercy that lifts the head.
There is a greatness for those who genuflect,
  and a majesty for the meek.
For the God who gave Himself is able
  to lift them up and lead them back.
With heads held high,
  they will walk in His Presence,
not as gods of chiseled stone,
  but souls cut of Heaven's cloth.
But what hope remains
  for the man of his own making,
  who blasphemes the Spirit
  as he clings to his altar of goodness?
Will the sword not claim him there?
  Will he not become the sacrifice
    on the stone table he has made?
It is a madness fit for the mad,
  who have traded Heaven for hell;
who have decided
  to walk past the torn curtain
  into their bottomless abyss.
But blessed is the man
  who washes in the blood, not water,
  and who comforts in the cross,
    not his convictions.
He is the man whose sins are covered
  in the depths of unfailing love—
and when he rises to breathe again,
  his breath will last forever.

Selected Readings for Further Study

† Isaiah 53:4-12

† Matthew 27:11-56

Questions for Reflection and Prayer:

1. What does it mean to live in rebellion to God? Do you see yourself as a rebel from birth? In many ways, our culture celebrates the "rebel." Does God share our enthusiasm for rebellion?

2. The nineteenth century German philosopher, Friedrich Nietzsche, galvanized contemporary godlessness when he declared:

> God is dead. God remains dead. And we have killed him. How shall we, the murderers of all murderers, comfort ourselves? What was holiest and most powerful of all that the world has yet owned has bled to death under our knives. Who will wipe this blood off us? What water is there for us to clean ourselves?...Is not the greatness of this deed too great for us? Must not we ourselves become gods simply to seem worthy of it? There has never been a greater deed; and whoever will be born after us—for the sake of this deed he will be part of a higher history than all history hitherto.

Was Nietzsche a prophet, a deluded fool, or a bit of both? What do you think God's final verdict will be for those who align themselves with Nietzsche's "theology"?

3. Existentialist philosopher, Jean-Paul Sartre, concludes his short story, "The Wall," with this memorable line: "I laughed so hard I cried." Do you think God ever looks at our world and does the same?

References
  Isa 48:8; 53:4-12; 59:13; Mt 27:16-26; Lk 23:34; 11:11-12; Eph 2:1-9

Diving Deeper:

1. J.D. Eubanks, MD, "Heads Held High" in *More of Him, Less of Me* (Dawn Treader, LLC, 2018), 80.
2. Friedrich Nietzsche, "The Gay Science" in *Existentialism from Dostoevsky to Sartre*, ed. Walter Kaufmann (New York: Plume, 1975), 126.
3. Jean-Paul Sartre, "The Wall" in *Existentialism from Dostoevsky to Sartre*, ed. Walter Kaufmann (New York: Plume, 1975), 299.

The Eleventh Hour

Psalm 32:3—When I kept silent,
    my bones wasted away
    through my groaning all day long.

O Lord, what mystery lies in silence,

that great space pregnant
    with the siblings of potential and uncertainty.
The wisest amongst us said,
    there is a time for everything,
even the soundless enigma
    in which God often resides.
Maybe the fool knows it too,
    and might blunder into wisdom
    when he holds his tongue.
For what great devilry comes
    of that unwieldly instrument!
How often the mouth fails
    more than it succeeds.
Even Jesus, in His perfection,
    chose to hold His tongue
    before His scheming accusers.
With a simple word,
    He might have silenced His enemies.
But though oppressed and afflicted,
    the Suffering Servant
    did not brandish His sword.
He was led like a lamb to the slaughter;
    like a silent sheep before the shearers,
    He did not unleash His fury.
He changed the world
    with the power of this silence.
But is there not also a time to speak,
    and a moment to step out
    into the quiet emptiness?
For what if Esther hid
    in the security of silence?
Would you have been pleased, Lord,
    with the selfish cowardice of her tongue?

42

Wasn't it right for her to speak
  what only she could speak?
And even you, Lord, have said,
  "I will not keep silent,
    for Jerusalem's sake I will not remain quiet,
    till her righteousness shines out like the dawn,
    her salvation like a blazing torch."
So with confidence I cry out to you;
  like your suffering seers,
    I cannot keep silent.
For to swallow my tongue in this time
  threatens to burst me;
and if I do not speak to you
    through the honesty of my anguish,
    how can I call you my Father and my Friend?
For you tell me,
  if I ask anything in your Name,
    I shall receive it.
If I'm wanting, am I a coward?
  Do I simply lack the courage
    to break the silence?
On the shore of your immensity, Father,
  I'll venture to dimple your silent depths
  with the pebbles of my petitions.
And though you know my words
  before anything tumbles off my tongue,
for the weakness of my faith's sake,
  show me you are listening to my pleas.
For I desperately long for you to speak
    into the air around me,
  like you spoke to your Beloved—
"This is my Son, whom I love;
  with Him I am well pleased."
Punctuate my silence, Father,
  with this show of paternal affection;
rescue me from the anguish
  of a deaf world
    that listens only to its own mantras.
Whisper your letters of love to me,
    until at last I arrive home
  into the embrace beyond words.

Selected Readings for Further Study

† Esther 4:1-17

† Matthew 26: 57-67

Questions for Reflection and Prayer:

1. Can you think of a time when you spoke hastily and perhaps the better option might have been to hold your tongue? How about a time when you chose to remain silent, and maybe, like Esther, you should have spoken up?

2. What does Jesus' silence before the Jewish leaders have to teach us? Why did He not choose to silence their insolence?

3. Prayer is the language of silence. It is listening to the discourse of Heaven. Kierkegaard describes the praying man:

> Something strange and wonderful happened to him: gradually, as he became more and more fervent in prayer, he had less and less to say, and finally he became silent. Indeed, he became what is, if possible, even more the opposite of talking than silence: he became a listener. He had thought that to pray was to talk; he learned that to pray is not only to keep silent, but to listen. And that is how it is: to pray is not to listen to oneself speak, but is to come to keep silent, and to continue keeping silent, to wait, until the person who prays hears God.

Has your prayer life moved from talking to listening? Have you permitted God to fill your silence with His divine communication?

References
Est 4:14; Job 7:11; Pr 17:28; Ecc 3:7; Isa 42:14; 53:7; 62:1; Jer 4:19; Mt 3:7; 7:7; 26:63; Acts 18:9; Jas 4:2

Diving Deeper:

1. J.D. Eubanks, MD, "Speaking Up" in *More of Him, Less of Me* (Dawn Treader, LLC, 2018), 133.
2. Søren Kierkegaard, *The Lily of the Field and the Bird of the Air* (Princeton, NJ: Princeton University Press, 2016), 19-20.

The Twelfth Hour

Psalm 32:4—For day and night
your [the Lord's] hand was heavy upon me;
my strength was sapped
as in the heat of summer.

What amazing power, O God,

lies in the hand of man—
that five-fingered instrument
through which we feel
the world around us!
By the hand, we clothe and feed ourselves;
we grasp the plow, wield the knife,
and cradle the suckling child.
In war, the hand may take a life;
in art, it may—in imitation of God—
create new worlds.
By the hand, the blind may see;
through the fingers,
the drowning may reach out for rescue.
And yet, what is the hand of man
compared to the hand of the Lord?
For has not your right hand, O God,
laid the foundations of the earth,
put the sun and moon in their place,
and formed humanity
from the dust of distant stars?
Has it not only created, but recreated—
stepped into that which it has made,
to plant the holy seed in virgin soil
and resurrect the righteous?
Yes, Lord, your hands are mighty;
they are as great as your Almighty Name!
For as the prophet reminds us,
by your hands you bring death and life;
by them, you wound and you heal;
no one can deliver us out of your hand.

~

45

Why then is your mighty hand
  now heavy upon me, O Lord?
Have *my* hands sinned against you?
  Have I wronged you
    like those Philistines
who placed your Holy Presence
  before the god of their own making?
Your hand was heavy upon them too;
  you afflicted them with tumors,
  and plagued them with panic.
Forgive me, Lord, for my own idolatry—
  for every attempt I make
    to place you in my curio,
      next to the other gods I have made.
Dare to lift your heavy hand
  from the neck of this small creature,
    who sometimes makes small of you, God.
Show me, instead, your hands of grace:
  the mercy that sustains,
  and the strength that upholds.

~

Lord, I confess my failure
  in the feeble legs of my faith.
I am too much of a Simon—
  full of desire to step out of the boat,
but leaden by doubt,
  instead of buoyed by faith.
Without you, I am foundering.
  Reach out your hand, Lord—
    catch your zealous friend.
Astride my wobbly legs,
    find a child's true heart;
  fill my weakness with your strength.
Be the shoulders upon which I sit,
  and the strong arms that hold me.
For though my heart's aim is child-true,
  its beat is sapped and sickly.
But you extend your open hands, Lord,
  full of a Father's love and favor.
So like the sinking Simon,
  give me the courage I need
  to open my hands to yours.

Selected Readings for Further Study

† Deuteronomy 32:39-43

† Matthew 14:22-36

Questions for Reflection and Prayer:

1. When was the last time you considered the creative power of God's hands? Can you picture your life held in the very hands that created the universe?

2. What does it mean when Job says, "…his [God's] hand is heavy…"(Job 23:2)? Do you feel that heaviness in your own life? If so, is it because God is testing you like He tested the righteous Job? Or, is that heavy hand a plague against your sin and the idolatry of your heart, much like it was for the Philistines?

3. Are you confident, deep down inside, that God's hands long to be merciful and gracious to you? Do you see Jesus reaching out to catch you like He did for Peter? Can you feel the loving touch His hand extended to the leper? Are your hands free to receive Christ's hands? Henri Nouwen leads us in the prayer of open hands:

> Dear God,
> I am so afraid to open my clenched fists!
> Who will I be when I have nothing left to hold on to?
> Who will I be when I stand before you with empty hands?
> Please help me to gradually open my hands
> and to discover that I am not what I own,
> but what you want to give me.
> And what you want to give me is love—
> unconditional, everlasting love.
> *Amen.*

References
Ex 9:3; 13:3; 15:6; 33:22-23; Dt 32:39; 1 Sam 5:1-12; Eze 8:22; Job 13:21; 23:2; Ps 37:24; 89:21; Isa 48:13; Mt 8:3; 14:31

Diving Deeper:

1. J.D. Eubanks, MD, "His Open Hands" in *More of Him, Less of Me* (Dawn Treader, LLC, 2018), 270.
2. Henri Nouwen, *With Open Hands* (Notre Dame: Ave Maria Press, 2006), 27.

Psalm 32:5—Then I acknowledged my sin to you [Lord]
and did not cover up my iniquity.
I said, "I will confess
my transgressions to the Lord"—
and you forgave
the guilt of my sin.

Heavenly Father, all too often

we are like that first couple in the Garden,
surrounded by an abundance
we cannot even enjoy,
because we are intent on hiding from you.
But what lasting pleasure can be found
lurking in these lonely shadows?
Wasn't the serpent wrong to say,
"You will not surely die"?
For death is exactly what has come—
the forbidden knowledge
that distanced me from you.
And of what worth is an enlightened life
separated from your Presence?
What if I gain the whole world,
yet lose my soul?
Jesus was tempted in the desert
with the kingdoms of the world.
But He refused the devil's bargain.
What then of me?
Have I truly become a man like Cain—
a coldblooded killer convinced
the blood will not cry out against me?
Have I turned a deaf ear to Isaiah's rebuke?
Can I not see the blood on my hands?
Has the tempter's delusion so fooled me
that I believe what is false?
The father of lies has planted
his prophets everywhere,
trying with twisted plots
to hide the irrepressible Light.

48

But can a city on a hill be hidden at night?
  Does the eclipsing moon erase the sun,
  or does the star burst forth in brilliance?
No! The City's light shines from a great distance,
  and nothing but your hand, God,
  shall forever blot out your sun.
We cannot hide from your radiance, Lord,
  for nothing in all creation is hidden
    from your sight.
Your eyes penetrate the shadows
  and lay us bare—
naked before the of gaze of Him
  to whom we must give account.
Therefore, I will confess my sin to you;
  I will open my mouth to repent.
For only in the soil of repentance
  will the true life take root—
    with confession of transgressions,
  the Kingdom's tendrils grow.
And you are faithful and just, Lord;
  you will forgive us our sins,
  and purify us of all unrighteousness.
We shall send down hungry roots
  to embed like a tree by streams of water—
    your mighty oaks of righteousness
  will rise into the sky.
In the knowledge of this hope,
  I will open my mouth.
I will confess with my tongue
  that Jesus is Lord,
and believe in my heart
  that God raised Him from the dead.
Then salvation will break my chains;
  the fetters of my soul will fall!
No longer a prisoner of my vices,
  I step out of my shadow-shackles,
    a willing slave of your righteousness.

49

Selected Readings for Further Study

† Genesis 3:1-13; 4:1-16

† 1 John 1:5-10

Questions for Reflection and Prayer:

1. Are you, like Adam and Eve, attempting to hide from God? Is there some "secret" sin you don't want Him to see? Have you convinced yourself His eyes don't penetrate the shadows?

Saint Augustine says, "The good man, though a slave, is free; the wicked, though he reigns, is a slave, and not the slave of a single man, but—what is far worse—the slave of as many masters as he has vices." Have you found the freedom of living within God's commands? Or, in your efforts to be "free," have you chosen to become a slave of your vices?

2. Have you, like Jesus, had your moment with the devil in the desert? If he has not yet come to offer you the "kingdoms of the world," know that he one day will. Will you be prepared to rebuke him as Jesus did?

3. Have you made confession before God a regular part of your life? Do you recognize that salvation hinges upon repentance? Of repentance, Martin Luther says, "Repentance is the *sadness* we experience after committing a specific sin as well as the *resolution* we then make not to sin in such a way again." Have you known this sadness? Have you resolved not to sin again? Can you hear God say, "Repent and live!" (Eze 18:32)? Are you determined to "walk in the light, as He [God] is in the light" (1 Jn 1:7)?

References
Ge 3:1-13; 4:1-16; Isa 1:15-16; 61:3; Da 9:7; Mt 4: 1-11; Ro 4:7; 10:9; 2 Thes 2:11-13; Heb 4:13-15; 1 Pe 2:16; 4:8; 1 Jn 1:9

Diving Deeper:

1. J.D. Eubanks, MD, "Oaks of Righteousness" in *More of Him, Less of Me* (Dawn Treader, LLC, 2018), 140.
2. Saint Augustine, *City of God* (New York: Penguin Books, 2003), 139.
3. Martin Luther, *Don't Tell Me That!* (Minneapolis, MN: Lutheran Press, 2004), 19.

The Fourteenth Hour

Psalm 32:6—Therefore let everyone who is godly
pray to you [Lord] while you may be found;
surely when the mighty waters rise,
they will not reach him.

O Lord, why is prayer
a ceaseless struggle,
as if it were an old and bitter enemy?
Must it be so hard
to speak to you from my heart?
For I know full well, Father,
that I pray too little,
and not often enough.
And even when I do pray,
are those feeble prayers
not like waves of the sea,
blown and tossed about
by the winds of doubt?
I hear your exhortations
to be faithful in prayer,
to pray continually, on all occasions,
and to never give up.
But how is this possible?
How can a man be constant
in anything, much less prayer?
Then I recall Samuel's warning—
"As for me, far be it from me
that I should sin against the Lord
by failing to pray…."
And despite his admonition,
fail I do!—time and time again.
Forgive me, Almighty God, I pray;
know my heart's desire,
even in the absence of articulation.
See in me a child who loves you,
even as he still struggles for words.

51

When I fumble in my speech,
  may your Spirit empower my weakness;
when I do not know what to pray for,
  may He intercede with groans
  that words cannot express.
May I remember how your Son
  taught us to pray;
 and when my prayers falter,
  may I recall the petitions of Scripture.
For I long, Lord, to be a warrior of prayer—
  a Moses who parts the sea,
an Elijah who summons fire from Heaven,
  and a Peter who raises the dead.
For were these men not men like me?
  Were they not also jars of clay?
Yet I stand amazed at how rough
  this poor vessel still is—
  how much work is yet to be done!
Mold me and make me, O Potter of men;
  form me into a vessel of your glory.
Help me, Lord, to become a man
  who, like your saints, wrestles—
  not *with* prayer, but *in* prayer—
a man who boldly puts on your full armor
  to stand against the schemes of Satan.
Steady my tumultuous sea;
  help me believe in the powerful plea—
  may my every breath trust in you.
May I seek you while you may be found,
  in this moment,
  amidst the darkness of this hour.
May I practice the presence of God,
  so that even my work and my silence
  become one long prayer to you.
Then, even when the mighty waters rise,
  you will be with me;
when I pass through the swollen rivers,
  they will not sweep over me.
For are you not the Lord, my God,
  the Holy One of Israel, my Savior,
  the Redeemer
  whose arm is mighty to save
  the man who trusts in you!

Selected Readings for Further Study

† 1 Samuel 12:1-25

† Matthew 6:1-13

Questions for Reflection and Prayer:

1. Have you realized, as the prophet Samuel recognizes, that a failure to pray is sin against God? Have you admitted, as Andrew Murray points out, "Our limited prayers, with the excuses we make for them, are a greater sin than we know"? Why do we so often fail to pray?

2. Jesus taught us to pray (Mt 6:9-13). Have you made the "Lord's Prayer" a regular part of your life? How can praying scriptural prayers inform and encourage our own prayers? Dietrich Bonhoeffer says, "Repeating God's own words after Him, we begin to pray to Him. We ought to speak to God and He wants to hear from us, not in the false and confused speech of our heart, but in the clear and pure speech which God has spoken to us in Jesus Christ." Are you praying this way?

3. What does Brother Lawrence mean when he encourages us to "practice the presence of God"? Have you reached the point in your prayer life where prayer has become what Brother Lawrence describes as:

>...an habitual, silent and secret conversation of the soul with God, which often causes me joys and raptures inwardly, and sometimes also outwardly, so great, that I am forced to use means to moderate them and prevent their appearance to others?

References
　　1 Sam 12:23; Isa 43:2; Mt 6:9-13; 21:22; Lk 18:1; Ro 8:26; 12:12; Eph 6:10-19; Col 4:12; 1 Thes 5:17; Jas 5:15-16; 1 Pe 3:12

Diving Deeper:

1. J.D. Eubanks, MD, "Failure to Pray" in *More of Him, Less of Me* (Dawn Treader, LLC, 2018), 55.
2. Andrew Murray, *The Ministry of Intercession* in *Collected Works on Prayer* (New Kensington: Whitaker House, 2013), 706.
3. Dietrich Bonhoeffer, *Psalms* (Minneapolis, MN: Augsburg, 1970), 11.
4. Brother Lawrence, *Practice the Presence of God* (Public Domain).

Psalm 32:7—You [Lord] are my hiding place;
you will protect me from trouble
and surround me with songs of deliverance.

W hen I consider

your servant David, O Lord,
I am reminded of your anointing—
the horn of oil that sets us apart,
forever identified with Heaven.
For David was the Lord's anointed,
the unlikely boy chosen to be king.
And yet, with the blessed unction
came bitter animosity;
with that oil, came the jealousy of men.
Hunted like an animal,
your anointed hid himself
in the Crags of the Wild Goats.
But did David not also hide himself in you?
Did he not cry out from the cave,
*"You are my refuge,
my portion in the land of the living"*?
Lord, you were the hiding place
of the budding king of Israel—
no less, the refuge of your Anointed One,
the coming King of Righteousness.
For while the Son of Man walked the earth,
was he not also hunted by men?
Your Anointed was pursued unto death;
the Holy One of Israel
was crucified like a common criminal.
Far be it from me, O God,
to expect anything less.
For shall I not be persecuted
as the Son was persecuted?
Shall I not suffer for the One who suffered,
and taste the hot pursuit of my enemy?

What is the alternative?
   To walk the broad road
   that makes a lie my refuge instead?
Would it be better to run from you, Lord,
   into the sea of vanishing pleasures
   and make falsehood my hiding place?
No, my Savior, you are my high tower,
   my refuge from the storms and rain.
You alone will set me high upon a rock
   and deliver me from the swirling waters—
from the enemies who seek to destroy me,
   and the exhaustion which threatens
      to unravel me.
For the dogged pursuit of the righteous,
   is as persistent as your call
      to the pursuit of righteousness, O Lord.
And if I do not, by your grace, persevere,
   shall I not be overcome
      by the hell-hounds nipping at my heels?
Therefore, the Son of Man prayed for me—
   not, as I sometimes desire,
that I might be taken out of the world—
   but that your shepherding hand, Father,
      might protect me from the evil one.
So I pray—reach out that hand, Lord,
   and hold me close to your strength;
gather me under your wings—
   let your plumage cover my helplessness.
For are you not the faithful God,
   the One who promises
      to strengthen and protect us?
Indeed, if only a small fraction
   of what you say is true,
      shall I not be blessed!
And yet—who can fathom it?—
   it is either all true, or it is not true at all—
      there is no in-between:
   on this wager, I risk everything.
For I have been claimed by your oil,
   and my cup overflows.
When I walk through the parted sea,
   teach me to sing the great song
      of your mighty deliverance.

<u>Selected Readings for Further Study</u>

† Exodus 15:1-18

† John 17:6-19

<u>Questions for Reflection and Prayer:</u>

1. Are you hiding *from* God or *in* God? Is your refuge a world of lies, or the Lord who created you and made you?

2. In her book, *Called, Appointed, Anointed,* singer and song-writer Janny Grien says, "Once you are called and appointed for the service God has called you to, you become a candidate for the anointing of God. This anointing is a special outpouring of the power of God to accomplish a task He appoints you to do." Have you received this special unction of God's Spirit? Have you been set apart for His purposes? What is He calling you to do?

3. C.S. Lewis says of Christianity, "One must keep on pointing out that Christianity is a statement which, if false, is of no importance, and, if true, of infinite importance. The one thing it cannot be is moderately important." If true, Christianity changes *everything*. But as Lewis points out, it cannot just be another religion filled with some "desirable" truths. Have you risked believing that no matter what "truths" may emerge in other religions, Christianity is the only religion which holds the *Truth*?

References
        Ex 15:1-18; 1 Sam 24; Isa 4:6; 28:15; Jn 17:11, 15; 2 Thes 3:3

<u>Diving Deeper:</u>

1. J.D. Eubanks, MD, "The Dissipated Heart" in *More of Him, Less of Me* (Dawn Treader, LLC, 2018), 348.
2. Janny Grien, *Called, Appointed, Anointed* (Tulsa, Oklahoma: Harrison House, 1996), 45.
3. C.S. Lewis, *God in the Dock* (Grand Rapids, MI: William E. Eerdman's Publishing Company, 1970), 102.

The Sixteenth Hour

Psalm 32:8—I will instruct you and teach you
in the way you should go;
I will counsel you and watch over you.

Wonderful Counselor, Mighty God,

Everlasting Father, Prince of Peace—
You are the great *Rabboni* who has come
    to teach us the way we should go.
You are the Way, for you are the Truth,
    and in this Truth alone there is life.
From the beginning, you have instructed us;
    you have given us your decrees.
And yet we, like sheep, have gone astray;
    we have wandered from your way.
Where would we be, Lord,
    if you were not as much Shepherd
        as you are Teacher?
What hope would I have for salvation,
    if you were not willing to leave
        the ninety-nine in search of me?
And how would I ever know you,
    if you did not speak your Word?
Thank you, Lord, for that Word,
    for it is a lamp to my feet
    and a light for my path.
Your Word shines in the darkness,
    and the darkness cannot overcome it.
For your Word reveals you, Lord,
    even as it generates from you;
within your Scripture lie the keys to life,
    and that Life is the Light of men.
O Teacher of men, you are the Word,
    the great *Logos* from the beginning,
    who was, and is, and is to come.
And though you have returned
    to your Father's side,

you have given us the Counselor,
the Spirit of all Truth.
Like a dove He descended from Heaven,
to rest the power of God on the Branch
and make that Vine bear His fruit.
For He is the Spirit of all wisdom
and understanding,
the Spirit of counsel and of power,
the Spirit of knowledge,
and of fear of the Lord.
And as He rested on the Branch,
so the Spirit desires to dwell
in the temple of man—
He in us, and we in Him.
The Spirit longs to guide us,
to instruct us in paths of righteousness.
Yet so often we cling to Babylon,
and blaspheme in our hearts
the Almighty Counselor of men.
We say, "*I will continue forever—*
I am, and there is none beside me."
Have our hearts not declared:
"*I will ascend to Heaven;*
I will raise my throne
above the stars of God—
I will ascend above the tops of the clouds;
I will make myself like the Most High"?
But will our waxen wings
carry us to these celestial heights?
Will they not betray us,
and prove our unteachable hearts worthy
to be brought down to the grave?
Forgive us, Lord, I pray,
for our unwillingness to bow.
Shepherd and Teacher, who stooped to make us great,
give us the gentle strength
to do as you have humbly done.
Spirit and Counselor, show us how to obey,
that in our obedience we may find your joy.
For the one who obeys you, O Lord,
remains in your love,
that your joy may be in him,
and his joy might be complete in you.

Selected Readings for Further Study

† Isaiah 11:1-9

† John 14:15-27

Questions for Reflection and Prayer:

1. Why is it important that Jesus was repeatedly called *Rabbi*, *Rabboni*, or *Teacher*? To the Pharisees, His teaching was an unorthodox and blasphemous "foolishness." But if Jesus' teaching had been "orthodox," would it have changed the world?

2. Christ's teachings come to us through His Word and the work of the Spirit. Are you reading His Word daily? Are you interacting with the Counselor? Is the third person of the Godhead your daily tutor? Is He living in you, and you in Him?

3. Thousands of years ago, the Greeks gave us the story of Icarus as a reminder of the costs of hubris. Why do we so often choose the ill-fated path of Icarus? Why do we strut about with the pride of Babylon?

German poet, Heinrich Heine, admits (in his autobiographical *Confessions*) to this Babylonian hubris in his youth: "I myself was the living law of morality, the source of all justice and authority. I was primal rectitude, I was incapable of sin, I was purity incarnate." Later on, however, God forces Heine to his knees, and the poet says, "Like many other ruined gods…I had to abdicate miserably and return to private life as a human being….I am no imitator of God. With holy humility I have given notice…that I am only a pitiful human being." Do you, like Heine, need to repent today of your willful desire to make yourself "God" of your own life?

References
> Job 12:13; Ps 73:24; 119:105; Isa 9:6; 11:1-9; 14:11-15; 47:1-15; Jer 38:15; Mic 4:2; Lk 12:12; Jn 1:38; 14:25; 15:9-11; 20:16

Diving Deeper:

1. J.D. Eubanks, MD, "Making Joy Complete" in *More of Him, Less of Me* (Dawn Treader, LLC, 2018), 211.
2. J.D. Eubanks, MD, "Joy: The Top of Heaven's Stairway" in *For the Joy of Obeying* (Dawn Treader, LLC, 2019), 77-83.
3. Heinrich Heine, *Confessions* (Joseph Simon Publishers, 1981), 47-49.

The Seventeenth Hour

Psalm 32:9—Do not be like the horse or mule,
which have no understanding,
but must be controlled by bit and bridle
or they will not come to you.

O *El Shaddai, Adonai,*

El Elyon, Elohim—
Almighty God, the great *I AM*—
what is man in the shadow of your Presence,
   the son of man, before your glory?
It is true, you have created us
   in the terrible beauty of your image.
We are gorgeous works of art,
   so breathtaking that we often delight
      in our reflected beauty,
   rather than you.
Forgive us, O Lord, I pray,
   for our reckless infatuations
      and our misguided affections.
We are easily enticed
   and quickly seduced.
Formed in beauty and strength,
   we were created to run your race;
like a horse in open country,
   to gallop free and not stumble.
But we have chosen our own courses
   and decided to rejoice in our strength,
   rather than the hands that formed it.
We have forgotten—your ways are not our ways,
   and your pleasure is not
      in the strength of the horse,
      nor your delight in the legs of a man.
Your joy falls upon hearts that fear you;
   you pleasure in those who put their hope
      in your unfailing love.
So what can Love do when willfully rejected,
   but place bit and bridle on unruly hearts?

60

Can the Father of compassion sit idly by,
　　while the child He has forged in love
　　　destroys himself in rebellion?
Love refuses to simply look away
　　and forever turn His back
　　　on my self-inflicted tragedy.
True Love strikes with blindness
　　as He meets me on my Damascus road.
His unfailing affection
　　brings me to my knees,
even as He feels the painful spike—
　　my constant kicking against the goads.
Thank you, Jesus, for your bit and bridle,
　　for the prods that bring the pain
　　　of an enlightened understanding.
For in this country east of Eden—
　　this land of lost innocence—
　　　we constantly lose our way.
We rebel against you,
　　strike out on our own,
　　and forget your great acts of mercy.
But thanks be to you, O gracious Lord,
　　that you rein us in;
in gentleness you guide us back
　　and lead us in paths of righteousness
　　　for your name's sake.
And one day, *Yahweh*,
　　you will forever remove
　　　this chaffing bit and bridle.
For on the glorious day
　　when the Rider of the White Horse
　　leads us home into your Presence,
no whip, halter, bit or bridle—
　　no reins will need to draw me to you—
for my eyes shall be opened,
　　my understanding perfected,
and I shall run to you, O Maker of Men,
　　with every ounce of who I am.

61

Selected Readings for Further Study

† Isaiah 63:7-14

† Luke 23:26-43

Questions for Reflection and Prayer:

1. God has many names, but there is only *one* God. Have you considered the names of God like the facets of a diamond? For He is—as poet-priest, G.M. Hopkins, calls Him—the "Immortal Diamond." And each name of God represents a different facet of His shining glory. Have you considered that multi-faceted glory?

2. Beauty is a blessing and a curse. God made things beautiful to draw our eyes to Him. But so often, we allow beauty to do just the opposite. How have you delighted in beauty rather than the One who made things beautiful? Can you begin using a delight in beauty as a tool to draw your eyes to Him?

3. Have you found yourself, like Saul of Tarsus on the road to Damascus, kicking against the goads of God? Can you envision a day when your heart and mind will be so in tune with the Lord's that you will not need any bit and bridle?

References
> Ge 17:1; Ex 3:13-15; Dt 6:4; Ps 33:17; 147:10; Pr 26:3; Isa 63:13; Zec 10:3; 12:4; Lk 23:34

Diving Deeper:

1. J.D. Eubanks, MD, "Kicking Against the Goads" in *More of Him, Less of Me* (Dawn Treader, LLC, 2018), 341.
2. Gerard Manley Hopkins, "That Nature is a Heraditian Fire and of the Comfort of the Resurrection," in *Poems of Gerard Manley Hopkins*, ed. W.H. Gardner and N.H. Mackenzie (Oxford, England: Oxford University Press, 1970), 106.
3. J.D. Eubanks, MD, "Immortal Diamond" in *Twelve Stones: Apologetics for an Age of Relativism* (Dawn Treader, LLC, 2022), 46-58.

The Eighteenth Hour

Psalm 32:10—Many are the woes of the wicked,
but the Lord's unfailing love
surrounds the man who trusts in Him.

I t is said, O God, love always trusts.

But does it? Should it?
For are you not love itself,
  and did Love entrust Himself to men?
Can even the holy ones be trusted?
  How much less these hearts of flesh?
Did not the angel of light
  betray you for the darkness?
Isn't there a bit of his treachery
  in the depths of every heart?
For you, O Lord, know our hearts,
  and you see no good in them.
Yet somehow, you love us still:
    the zealous disciple
      who denied you three times;
    the king who plotted, murdered
      and slept with the wife of another;
    the surly prophet who ran from you
      as he boarded a ship for Tarshish;
    and a nation that repeatedly bowed
      to gods of wood and stone—
somehow, you loved them all,
  just as you love me.
Father, yours is an amazing love,
  full of an unfailing forbearance!
It surrounds and protects
  the one who trusts in you.
Jesus was surrounded by your love,
  for He is Love,
    and He is one with you.
In Christ's life and death,
  He showed us how to trust in you.

For who can imagine the trust
   that caused Him to leave your side,
to trade His throne for the flesh of men,
   His perfect Kingdom for a world of ruin?
Who can fathom the depth of His faith in you,
   that caused Him to bow to your will,
as He suffered the blows of men
   and hung as a curse on a tree?
His enemies jested at the faith holding Him there—
     "He trusts in God.
        Let God rescue him if He wants him."
But it was His love and steadfast peace
   that fixed Him in the air.
In quietness and trust,
   Christ found His strength in you.
He did not lean upon His own understanding;
   He was not foolish enough
     to trust in Himself.
Jesus did not attempt to light His own torch
   and walk by the illumination
     of His own counsel.
Even in His darkest hour,
   Christ trusted in the Name of the Lord—
     He relied on His Father's wisdom.
The Son's confidence was in you, O Lord,
   for He knew His reward was with God.
Even as He cried out,
   "Eloi Eloi, lama sabachthani,"
     Christ trusted in Heaven's will.
Give me, Father, I pray,
   the confidence of Christ.
May I trust you with the faith of Jesus,
   the Savior who lives in me.
Though my neighbor may not be trustworthy,
   though my closest friend may betray me,
and the one who lies in my embrace forsake me,
   you will not forsake me, O Lord.
For while the wicked and righteous alike
   may face troubles of many kinds,
the one who puts his trust in you
   will never be shaken.
For the God who is unfailing Love has said,
   "Never will I leave you, never will I forsake you."

<u>Selected Readings for Further Study</u>

† Isaiah 26:1-10; 50:10-11

† Matthew 27:32-55

<u>Questions for Reflection and Prayer:</u>

1. Trust is an essential component of every relationship. And yet, we must be careful in our dispensation of trust in others, and even in ourselves. Why? Oswald Chambers says, "You should trust no one, and even ignore the finest saint on earth if he blocks your sight of Jesus Christ." For trust, like everything else, must bow before Jesus. Is your trust bowing before Jesus?

2. Is it possible to be wary with trust and still love? Can we love with the love of Christ without entrusting ourselves to men? How does Jesus perfectly execute love to everyone, even those who openly malign and betray Him?

3. As the life of Jesus shows us, though men may fail us, God does not. And the one who trusts in His unfailing love, will find steadfast peace, quietness of soul, and strength of spirit. Has your trust in God brought you to this special place? If not, why?

References
> Dt 31:6-8; Job 4:18; 15:15; Ps 9:10; 20:7; 33:21; Pr 3:5; 28:26; Isa 26:3; 30:15; 49:4; 50:10; Mic 7:5; Mt 27:43; 1 Cor 13:7

<u>Diving Deeper:</u>

1. J.D. Eubanks, MD, "Loving Through to Trust" in *More of Him, Less of Me* (Dawn Treader, LLC, 2018), 244.
2. J.D. Eubanks, MD, "Saved in Rest, Strengthened in Quietness" in *More of Him, Less of Me* (Dawn Treader, LLC, 2018), 147.
3. J.D. Eubanks, MD, "Quiet Confidence: The Stabilizing Trunk of Gentleness" in *Gentlest of Ways* (Dawn Treader, LLC, 2020), 45-66.
4. Oswald Chambers, *My Utmost for His Highest* (Grand Rapids, MI: Discovery House Publishers, 1992), March 29.

The Nineteenth Hour

Psalm 32:11—Rejoice in the Lord and be glad, you righteous;
sing, all you who are upright.

Spring, O God, is a constant chorus
 of rejoicing to you—
the birds on greening boughs
 sing their songs
 to the soft tempo of gentle rain;
the flowers unfurl their petals of praise,
 like velvet arms before a sea
 of robin-egg blue;
and the barren trees' blossoms burst forth
 from tightly bound buds,
to flame out pastel hills
 and augur the million engines of living.
All creation rejoices in you, O Lord,
 Author and Perfecter of all things.
For you are its firstborn,
 and by you, for you alone,
 everything was created—
things in Heaven and on earth,
 invisible and visible,
whether the distant nebulas,
 or the far reaches of my heart.
This surge of living is an exaltation
 the righteous cannot ignore,
for it sings with the Spirit's exuberance
 and carols the Father's joy.
Forgive me then, O Lord,
 for my winter months,
for those days of bleak darkness,
 and sometimes deathly silence,
when I do forget your praise
 and neglect to honor your glory.
For your glory is your goodness;
 when I fail to remember your goodness,
 I softly scorn your glory.

In these seasons of cold austerity,
  help me recall your lovingkindness.
May I rejoice in your promises
  and be glad in your salvation.
For shall I not sing with the Daughter of Zion,
    and shout aloud with Jerusalem,
to the One who has taken away my punishment
  and defeated my mortal enemy?
Shall I not rejoice and be glad
  and give Him glory,
this Lamb who has come
  and taken away the sin of the world,
to prepare His bride for the wedding
  of His final, triumphal return?
Spring delights in this coming victory,
  even as its singers quickly fade.
Each member of Heaven's passing chorus
  heralds the Creator's *poietic*[7] power
    and the Savior's salvific work.
In every dancing atom,
  His trumpet-clad messengers
remind us to give thanks in all things,
  to rejoice in the Lord always,
    in every circumstance, of every day.
In their vernal chorus they are the teachers,
  and we those slow disciples,
who standing in the presence of a King,
  fail to see the crown upon His head.
Forgive us, Lord, for our blindness;
  do not hold our muteness against us.
Open our eyes, Savior, so they might see,
  the easter you have brought
    to our desolate darkness.
Touch our lips, God, that they might sing
  the praises due your Almighty Name.
Great Spirit, be the eternal spring in me—
  the power that draws
    your sap of living up
into the farthest reaches
  of my barren boughs.

---

[7] In philosophical language, *poiesis* refers to the creative power by which one brings something into existence that did not exist before.

Selected Readings for Further Study

† Zephaniah 3:14-20

† Philippians 4:4-7

Questions for Reflection and Prayer:

1. The Psalmist says, "Let the heavens rejoice, let the earth be glad…"(Ps 96:11). What does creation have to sing about? Can you see and hear the rejoicing of God's universe? And if not, why?

2. Every life that is honestly lived has moments of bleakness and darkness akin to the winter months. But God has given us spring as a reminder of His resurrecting power. The poet, G.M. Hopkins, says, "Let him [Christ] easter in us, be a dayspring to the dimness of us, / be a crimson-cresseted east…." Have you allowed the colors of spring to focus your heart on Christ's reclamation of your life?

3. God tells Moses that His goodness is His glory (Ex 33:18-19). As pastor Dane Ortlund reminds us, "When we speak of God's glory, we are speaking of who God is, what He is like, His distinctive resplendence, what makes God *God*. And when God Himself sets the terms on what glory is, He surprises us….His glory is His goodness." Have you employed God's goodness in your life as a tool to bring you to rejoice in His glory? Have you taken a moment to give thanks today for the garden of goodness God has placed you in?

References
>   Dt 12:18; Ex 33:18-19; Ps 96:1113; 119:14, 62; Isa 9:3; 13:3; 25:9; 35:1;
>   Hab 3:18; Zep 3:14-17; Php 4:4; Col 1:15-16; 1 Thes 5:16; Rev 19:7

Diving Deeper:

1. J.D. Eubanks, MD, "Garden of Goodness" in *More of Him, Less of Me* (Dawn Treader, LLC, 2018), 130.
2. Gerard Manley Hopkins, "The Wreck of the Deutschland" in *Poems of Gerard Manley Hopkins*, ed. W.H. Gardner and N.H. Mackenzie (Oxford, England: Oxford University Press, 1970), 63.
3. Dane Ortlund, *Gentle and Lowly: The Heart of Christ for Sinners and Sufferers* (Wheaton, IL: Crossway, 2020), 147.

III.

Psalm 38

A psalm of David. A petition.

O Lord, do not rebuke me in your anger
  or discipline me in your wrath.
For your arrows have pierced me,
  and your hand has come down upon me.
Because of your wrath there is no health in my body;
  my bones have no soundness because of my sin.
My guilt has overwhelmed me
  like a burden too heavy to bear.
My wounds fester and are loathsome
  because of my sinful folly.
I am bowed down and brought very low;
  all day long I go about mourning.
My back is filled with searing pain;
  there is no health in my body.
I am feeble and utterly crushed;
  I groan in anguish of heart.
All my longings lie open before you, O Lord;
  my sighing is not hidden from you.
My heart pounds, my strength fails me;
  even the light has gone from my eyes.
My friends and companions avoid me
    because of my wounds;
  my neighbors stay far away.
Those who seek my life set their traps,
  those who would harm me talk of my ruin;
  all day long they plot deception.
I am like a deaf man, who cannot hear,
  like a mute man, who cannot open his mouth;

I have become like a man who does not hear,
  whose mouth can offer no reply.
I wait for you, O Lord;
  you will answer, O Lord my God.
For I said, "Do not let them gloat
    or exalt themselves over me when my foot slips."
For I am about to fall,
  and my pain is ever with me.
I confess my iniquity;
  I am troubled by my sin.
Many are those who are my vigorous enemies;
  those who hate me without reason are numerous.
Those who repay my good with evil
  slander me when I pursue what is good.
O Lord, do not forsake me;
  be not far from me, O my God.
Come quickly to help me,
  O Lord, my Savior.

The Twentieth Hour

Psalm 38:1-2—O Lord, do not rebuke me in your anger
or discipline me in your wrath.
For your arrows have pierced me,
and your hand has come down upon me.

W ho, O Lord, can bear your anger?

Who can fathom your wrath?
For to think of your retribution
  melts the heart like wax;
to meditate on your anger,
  is to stand naked before the sun.
Nahum was right to ask,
  "Who can withstand His indignation?
  Who can endure His fierce wrath?"
For shall your anger against wickedness
  not pour out like molten fire,
    and the rocks become liquid before your fury?
You, God, are a mighty warrior
  before whom no one can stand.
Your mouth is like a sharpened sword;
  and you came not to bring a paltry peace,
    but a two-edged blade.
You are a polished arrow
  in the hands of the Archer
    who never misses His mark.
Your flame-tip justice flashes like lightening
  to pierce the heart of the one you love—
but it strikes with deadly force,
  the enemy who profanes your Almighty Name.
And though we, like Ahab before us,
  might disguise ourselves in suits of armor,
    your arrow always finds the chink.
No wonder the wicked jettison your wrath,
  and your enemies downplay your retribution.
For in merely considering your anger,
  are your foes not already vanquished?

71

Even some who sing your Holy Name
    dare to disavow your wrath,
as if Love must not possess anger,
    and the God who is jealous for our affections
        should not take *all* measures
    to make us His own.
Thank you, Lord, for being the arrow
    that pierces me to the marrow,
the double-edged sword that penetrates,
    even to dividing soul and spirit.
For if you did not wound me
        with the thrusts of your loving anger,
    how could I ever be yours?
If I never bled from the tip of your wrath,
    how would I ever know your healing love?
Yet I am saved only in this,
    that your anger against me lasts only a moment,
        but your favor a lifetime;
and though weeping may remain for a night,
    rejoicing comes in the morning.
For have you, my Savior, not borne
    the full force of God's wrath?
Has your blood not reconciled my rebellion
    and rescued me from certain death?
Though your hand, Lord,
        is now heavy upon me,
    I stand before you boldly,
        dressed in gleaming white.
Through your suffering I have been justified;
    by faith in your sacrifice,
I have gained access into the grace
    by which I now stand—
        forever!
In this grace, I rejoice in the hope of glory,
    even as I labor through these tears
        to give thanks in my afflictions.
Grant, O Lord, that I may see
    in suffering, perseverance;
    in perseverance, character;
        and in character, hope.
For your hope alone will not disappoint us;
    and faith shall not prove vain
        before Kingdom perseverance.

Selected Readings for Further Study

† 1 Kings 22:29-40

† Romans 5:1-11

Questions for Reflection and Prayer:

1. How has your life been like Ahab's? What suits of armor have you attempted to put on in an effort to hide from the arrows of God?

2. Have you ever thought of God as a warrior (Ex 15:3)? Many like the image of a gentle and peaceful Jesus. But have you considered Christ said He came to bring a sword, not peace? Have you pictured Him, as the Apostle John portrays Him in Revelation, as a conquering, warrior King? Why does this role matter?

3. Does the biblical God—not the God of the contemporary imagination—possess both love and wrath? Are they mutually exclusive, or does real Love, the Father's love, require the justice of His wrath? A.W. Tozer says, "The instructed Christian knows that the wrath of God is a reality, that His anger is as holy as His love, and that between His love and His wrath there is no incompatibility." How can this truth help you appreciate God's love even more?

References
Ex 15:3; Dt 32:23; 1 Ki 22:29-40; Job 6:4; Ps 7:12-13; 77:17; Isa 49:2; La 3:12-13; Na 1:6; Zec 9:14; Ro 5:1-11

Diving Deeper:

1. J.D. Eubanks, MD, "Chink in Your Armor" in *More of Him, Less of Me* (Dawn Treader, LLC, 2018), 41.
2. A. W. Tozer, *Man The Dwelling Place of God* (Public Domain).

The Twenty-first Hour

Psalm 38:3-4—Because of your [the Lord's] wrath there is no health in my body;
my bones have no soundness because of my sin.
My guilt has overwhelmed me
like a burden too heavy to bear.

I am a burdened man—

self-beset or bedeviled?—
a pilgrim with a pack that weighs me down.
Perhaps my guile is guilty,
and the load I lug on my back,
the just penance
for my heart's artifice.
But maybe my weight
has divine design,
and you've stuffed my sack, O Lord,
with stones enough
to weary my legs into a bow.
Maybe the sword that pierces my side
is the harbinger
of Heaven's healing power.
Perhaps the thorn that tears my flesh
is the unlikely instrument
of the unfathomable Good—
and the pain the rose's point brings,
the only path to Heaven's deepest pleasure.
Yet, there is no escaping the fact:
my sins outnumber
the hairs on my head;
my guilt stands before me,
taller than a glaring Goliath.
For sin is that sinkhole of the soul
that drinks a man down to the dregs;
and apart from the grasp of Grace,
it swallows us whole.
Even the ground beneath my feet
seems to reel like a drunkard,
so heavy upon it is the guilt of rebellion,
that it will one day fall—
never to rise the same again.

74

Will the dust of my days join this destiny, Lord?
   Must I make the one-way descent,
   from sickness to suffering to death?
Perhaps there is nothing beyond the grave.
   Maybe it is all as they say:
      dust to dust, and nothing more—
   a dissolution of random atoms.
Crowds bow before
   the perverse grace of chance,
   believing in guilt's denial.
So why not live
   in the populous delusion,
   when I can dress my conscience in white robes
      and forget the blood on my hands?
Why admit to the sordidness of sin,
   if it's only a subjective sickness
   the shaman's cheap charades
      can heal with a pile of pills?
For who wants to change their life,
   if they don't have to?
Who wants to admit guilt,
   if they can claim innocence instead?
But your voice, O Lord,
   thunders through today's therapeutic,
your prophets hammer home
      the guilt of the greedy
   and the culpability of our cupidity.
So when Heaven's lightening strikes,
   how shall we stand?
What would we do without the Man
   who walks toward us through the flames—
   the great Healer of the heart,
      who comes for the sickness of our souls!
His hands reach for the gutters,
      for the guilty—like me—lurking there,
   and for every other pilgrim
      with a burden too heavy to bear.
And with a smile He says,
   "Take my yoke upon you,
      for it is as light as a feather";
and the guilt I once knew,
   is swallowed in the updraft of Heaven.

<u>Selected Readings for Further Study</u>

† Isaiah 1:2-16

† Matthew 9:9-13

<u>Questions for Reflection and Prayer:</u>

1. Have you ever pictured yourself as John Bunyan's Christian—a weary pilgrim with a pack on his back? Have you ever felt the weight of your sin? Have you experienced the joy of feeling that pack fall from your back?

2. Some contemporary physicists, like Brian Greene, look at creation's incredible complexity and see nothing but "the grace of random chance." How does this worldview benefit them in the here and now? How will it hurt them in the days to come?

3. Christ said, "It is not the healthy who need a doctor, but the sick" (Mt 9:12). When He made this distinction, Jesus was not referring to physical illness, but to spiritual sickness. And yet, as philosopher Charles Taylor points out, contemporary culture has objectified morality into the "therapeutic register." In other words, "What was formerly sin is often now seen as sickness. This is the 'triumph of the therapeutic'…." Why burden ourselves with original sin, if it is just a sickness? Who needs salvation, if we can be treated by experts and pills? Have you slid into the "therapeutic register," or have you allowed Jesus to be the physician of your mortally sick soul?

References
> Lev 14; Eze 9:6-7; Isa 1:2-16; 6:6-7; 24:20; Jer 3:13; Mt 9:12 Ro 8:18; 2 Cor 12:7

<u>Diving Deeper:</u>

1. J.D. Eubanks, MD, "Highways of the Heart" in *More of Him, Less of Me* (Dawn Treader, LLC, 2018), 158.
2. Brian Greene, *Until the End of Time* (New York: HarperCollins, 2009), 94.
3. Charles Taylor, *A Secular Age* (Cambridge, MA: The Belknap Press, 2007), 618.

The Twenty-second Hour

Psalm 38:5—My wounds fester and are loathsome
because of my sinful folly.

King of Heaven, your wisest of men said,
  "the folly of fools yields folly."
But who is the fool, and what is folly?
  Is the jester the halfwit,
  or the deluded, disingenuous pundit?
Isn't the knowing down,
  who plays his part, as a part,
wiser than the royal sage,
  who in filling his august role,
  runs amok of his own counsel?
No doubt, Nabal was a Fool from birth.
  For didn't folly delight him
    who spurned God's anointed?
Yet, was the anointed any less foolish?
  Wouldn't David have lashed out in anger,
    but for the staying wisdom
    of a woman's diplomacy?
And what shall we say of the bejeweled king,
  who in wisdom built God's Temple
  and penned countless proverbs?
Though the breadth of his understanding
  stretched out like sand on the shore;
though he taught about animals and birds,
  and described the wonders of the world;
did his vision not extend to his own recesses—
  to the crags and nooks of his heart?
Was he not the greatest of fools,
  who in helping to pen God's Word,
  willfully transgressed its very commands,
as he held fast in loving embrace
  the perfumed multitude of nations?
And did not Christ profess six woes
  against the robes and tassels
    of Israel's teachers?

For what wisdom lies in dutiful tithes
   uncoupled from justice and love?
What hope remains for those tyrants
   who have taken away the key of knowledge—
the robes whose self-righteousness stands
   blocking the door to understanding?
Do they not know? Have they not seen?
   Does their blindness blind them to themselves?
For all are fools who have sinned
    and gone astray.
There is no one righteous, not even one;
   all men are capable of all things.
O Lord, though it pains me to admit it,
  I am too much a dog
    who returns to his own vomit.
And if it were not for your grace,
  would my foolishness
    not lead me to my own ruin?
For even the philosophers know,
  the only fool is the man
    who does not know he is a fool.
And the true dolt is not the ass,
   but the fool who believes himself wise,
    and a law unto himself.
Lord, forgive me for my self-governance,
   and for every attempt I make
   to live in the illusions of my sinful folly.
Thank you, Almighty God, for choosing
   to destroy the wisdom of the wise,
    and frustrate the council of the intelligentsia.
Thank you for the divine foolishness
   by which I am saved—
for the omniscience that bound itself
  in the babbling of a baby,
and the omnipotence that surrendered
  to hang by nails and gasp for breath.
When I consider it, shall I not be a fool
  for such a One as this,
who in ransom died for my living death,
  and then rose again,
    that I too might choose to rise?
I am no king, counselor, or sage.
  But I am a fool for Christ.

<u>Selected Readings for Further Study</u>

† 1 Samuel 25

† 1 Corinthians 1:18-25

<u>Questions for Reflection and Prayer:</u>

1. Commenting on Roman farcical drama, Saint Augustine says, "When those involved are actors and know what they are doing, it gets a well-deserved laugh in the theatre; when they are fools, who do not know what they are about, it is treated with more justified scorn in the real world." As Augustine points out, some people play the "fool," some people are fools, and others do some foolish things.
What does the story of Nabal and David have to teach us about "foolishness"? Does foolishness come in one variety or many? How can we, like Abigail, help one another in our folly?

2. King Solomon may be one of the Bible's greatest contradictions. Why? What does the incredible foolishness in the "wisest" of men have to teach us for our own lives? Do we have blind spots like Solomon?

3. Why did God create a story of salvation for humanity so riddled with apparent foolishness? What does Jesus have to say about this topic when He quotes Isaiah (Mt 13:11-17)? How can that which appears to defy reason on so many levels prove itself to be the only thing which is in fact reasonable?

References
      1 Sam 25; 1 Ki 4:29-34; Job 42:8; Pr 5:23; 14:24; 15:21; 17:12; 19:3; 24:9; 26:11; Lk 11:37-54; 1 Cor 1:18-34

<u>Diving Deeper:</u>

1. J.D. Eubanks, MD, "The Praise of Folly" in *More of Him, Less of Me* (Dawn Treader, LLC, 2018), 114.
2. Saint Augustine, *City of God* (New York: Penguin Books, 2003), 227.

79

The Twenty-third Hour

Psalm 38:6-8—I am bowed down and brought very low;
    all day long I go about mourning.
My back is filled with searing pain;
    there is no health in my body.
I am feeble and utterly crushed;
    I groan in anguish of heart.

Thank you, Lord, for your crushing blow,

for the strong hand that forced me down.
Thank you for knocking me to my knees
    in a tear-drenched darkness
        that screamed me into submission,
long before you come in the blinding
    light of your gleaming white—
one hand full of grace for the bowed,
    the other with smiting justice for the proud.
Thank you, God, for softly crushing
    the early fruit of my life
        in the winepress of your unending love,
so the sweet juice of your redeeming work
    might gladden the hearts of your people.
How grateful I am to be your work of art,
    a jar of clay broken to pieces
        by the gentleness of your pained reproach.
For are you not close to the brokenhearted?
    Do you not save those crushed in spirit?
Are you not crushed when I am crushed,
    and do you not mourn when I mourn?
You chose to be oppressed for me
    and to suffer for those chained in suffering.
O Lord, you willingly aligned yourself
    with the downtrodden.
With the shattered spirit, humbly bowed,
    you have decided to make your home.
Therefore, I welcome the brokenness
    that brings your indwelling.

But what hope remains for the uncrushed,
    for the heart that refuses to be rent
        and the knees that will not bow?
Shall the Stone not fall on the unrepentant?
    Those who abjure your Holy Name, Lord,
        shall they not be ground to dust?
The pieces of my soul you can, and do, reclaim;
    and the new vessel you form
        is filled with your living water.
You are the endless water, O Lord;
    and after the suffering of your soul,
        your liquid rose into the Light of life.
You opened the gates of Heaven,
    so your resurrecting radiance might fall
        en force
    on souls genuflected.
For the broken and contrite spirits
    will not see the second death;
and those who have died with you
    will rise alongside you,
        to reign in the light of your glory.
But your Stone separates the chaff;
    the husks will be blown by the wind
        and consumed by the fire.
For the God of peace will crush
    Satan under our feet;
the devil will be thrown,
    with the chaff he claims,
        into the roiling sulfur.
From the death of Death none escape,
    save those whose names
        are written in Heaven's ledgers.
So I thank you, Lord, for the bloody pen
    that has scribbled my name beneath yours.
Thank you, Father, for the crimson tide
    of your precious Scribe,
whose pierced flow has inked me
    into your eternal Presence.
I am beautifully broken, but claimed.
    I have been crushed, but made into wine.
For it is no longer I who live,
    but Christ who lives in me.

<u>Selected Readings for Further Study</u>

† Psalm 34:17-22

† Revelation 20:4-6; 21:6-8

<u>Questions for Reflection and Prayer:</u>

1. Have you ever felt crushed? Has the wrecking ball of life brought you to your knees? Is it possible that the God you say you believe in is behind that wrecking ball? Why does that matter?

2. Chinese gospel preacher, Watchman Nee, says the following:

> Everything that comes our way is meaningful and under God's sovereign arrangement. Nothing accidental happens to a Christian. Nothing is outside God's ordering. We have to humble ourselves under God's sovereign arrangements. May the Lord open our eyes to see that God is arranging everything around us; He has a purpose in us. Through everything He is *crushing* us.

Nee recognizes the importance of divine "crushing." Grapes do not become wine without crushing. Are our spiritual lives any different? Why does it matter that God was crushed for you?

3. Paul tells us in his letter to the Philippians "that at the name of Jesus every knee should bow, in Heaven and on earth and under earth" (2:9-10). Have you decided to bow? What lies in wait for those who, like Satan, refuse to bow?

References
Lev 2:14; Job 6:9; 9:17; 16:12; Ps 34:18; Isa 53:10; Jer 8:21; Mt 21:44; Lk 3:17; Ro 16:20; Gal 2:20; Rev 20:4-6; 21:6-8

<u>Diving Deeper:</u>

1. J.D. Eubanks, MD, "Nothing But Fragments" in *More of Him, Less of Me* (Dawn Treader, LLC, 2018), 138.
2. Watchman Nee, *The Breaking of the Outer Man and the Release of the Spirit* (Anaheim, CA: Living Stream Ministry, 1997), 39.

The Twenty-fourth Hour

Psalm 38:9—All my longings lie open before you, O Lord;
my sighing is not hidden from you.

This, O Lord, is the last frontier,
my wilderness of longing and desire.
It is an uncharted wilds
your eyes alone have seen—
a rugged country, unsearched and unknown:
a blank map of an indescribable territory,
filled with my guttural roars,
and the eerie, lonesome howls
of a heart that desperately hungers
to claim it and keep it all as its own.
In its wild and untamed interior,
I imagine my land of desire
impenetrable to your gaze,
enrobed in a sylvan shroud that hides
the midnight meanderings of my mind.
Yet what do sorties in the darkness bring,
but the straining eyes of a heart
growing weary with more longing,
till its orbs are two dull stones set in a weathered rock,
bracing the wind as they teeter on despair?
Such is the curse you foretold for the wayward will,
and the wicked price one pays, Lord,
for swallowing your blessings too quickly.
Because of the ravenous like me,
you parceled out your Promised Land,
little by little,
lest the feast prove too much to digest,
and the howling desert return
to claim the ripening fruits of your country.
For far too often I am dragged away
and enticed by my evil desires—
driven, not by the Spirit, but by my appetites.
The longings of the flesh often overrule
my longing for your commands.

83

Forgive me, Lord, for this dark transposition—
    for willfully not willing your will.
Do not, I pray, hold against me
    every fleeting desire
that chases your Name and renown
    from the yearnings of my heart.
Thank you for the godly sorrow you bring,
    ushering with it as it does,
        a longing to replace my longings—
a desire replete with repentance, filled with earnestness,
    and hungry, not for a doomed and empty independence,
        but the bondage that brings freedom.
For where once I growled, I now groan,
    not with the despair I ran from,
but a divine cocktail of ecstasy and hope—
    a longing to be clothed in my heavenly dwelling,
where the nakedness of my willful wildness
    finds covering in the building from God.
So my heart longs for the better country,
    for the home that houses my glory,
and for the company of those saints
    who dared to cling to faith
        amidst sighs, cries, and remonstrations.
My sighs you have heard, Lord;
    my cries you have felt;
        and my anger you have absolved.
But is there not a price to pay for this blessing,
    though the cost is small against eternity?
For you, not me, must be Captain of this soul—
    nothing costs nothing, and everything means everything.
So my partitioning must end here,
    where the illusions of sovereignty and secret
    die in the wilderness of desire—
        for you demand that territory too.
O Lord, I am now wholly captive
    in your train of love, a willing servant
        marching behind a King who owns it all.
And I thank you, God, for your patient siege—
    for the great battering ram of your grace
that broke through the walls
    of my last outpost,
to claim me from the rubble
    as your own.

Selected Readings for Further Study

† Isaiah 26:7-12

† 2 Corinthians 5:1-5

Questions for Reflection and Prayer:

1. Does becoming a disciple of Christ cost nothing, everything, or a bit of both? Dietrich Bonhoeffer says discipleship is costly to the disciple because "it compels a man to submit to the yoke of Christ and follow Him...." What has following Jesus cost you? What was the last piece of territory you had to cede to your King? Or, have you yet to give it up? Can you be a true disciple at no personal cost?

2. Thomas Merton says, "I might still go through life conforming myself to certain indications of God's will without ever fully giving myself to God. For that, in the last analysis, is the real meaning of His will. He does not need our sacrifices, He asks for our selves." What does it mean to will the will of God? Have you given yourself fully to God?

3. What is "godly sorrow" and how is it different than "worldly sorrow"? Why is godly sorrow important? How can God use it to transform our longings?

References
> Dt 28:65; Ps 40:8; 119:20, 81, 113; Pr 11:23; 13:12, 19; Isa 26:7-12; Hos 6:6; Ro 7:18; 1 Cor 12:31; 2 Cor 5:1-5; 7:10-11; 1 Thes 2:17; Heb 11:16; Jas 1:14; 2 Pe 2:10

Diving Deeper:

1. J.D. Eubanks, MD, "A Better Country" in *More of Him, Less of Me* (Dawn Treader, LLC, 2018), 110.
2. J.D. Eubanks, MD, "Invictus" in *More of Him, Less of Me* (Dawn Treader, LLC, 2018), 354.
3. Dietrich Bonhoeffer, *The Cost of Discipleship* (New York: Touchstone, 1995), 145.
4. Thomas Merton, *No Man is an Island* (New York: Houghton Mifflin Harcourt, 1983), 63.

The Twenty-fifth Hour

Psalm 38:10—My heart pounds, my strength fails me;
even the light has gone from my eyes.

Your greatest command, O Lord,

is to love you with all my heart,
and with all my soul, and all my strength.
But who can give you everything at every turn?
Where is the man who can both cease to exist,
and exist completely, all at once, in full intensity?
Is this not a bit like asking the sun to arrest forever
in the brightness of its midday glory?
For surely it is at noon that the sun does best
what you designed it to do:
illuminate the world you have made.
Do you not also ask this of me—
to be a light that burns brightly for you,
never dimming, never fading,
forever in an apogee of praise?
Forgive me then, O God, for my flickering;
do not count against me the faintness of my eyes.
If I were the sun, I would ceaselessly burn for you.
But I am nothing more than a broken man,
tending a small, smoldering fire.
Can mere embers produce the heat you desire?
Or must your Spirit fan those coals into a holy flame?
Maybe then I would reach out to you with all that I am.
Once, O Lord, you listened to man
to stop the sun in the middle of the sky.
Instead of continuing its ceaseless march,
the star hung for a pregnant moment
in the apex of its strength—
a blinding light by which you fought
with your people, for your people.
There has never been a day like it before or since,
when the sun did most fully what you called it to do,
as you halted the heavens by your power,
before the audacious words of a man.

86

But when the solar champion returned
　to running his endless course,
was he any less the sun,
　in the waxing and waning of his light?
On days when he now hides behind
　a deep blanket of clouds,
or reaches into the unknown darkness
　to bring brilliance to the world's far corners,
is he not still doing his best,
　shining his bit of your consuming fire?
And is the sun not perhaps most loved
　in his half-light moments,
　　when the borders of his strength cede soft beauty?
In all lights, the sun is still your glorious creation,
　called as he is to burn for you,
　　even as his mortal fire slowly dies.
I too am the stuff of stars, Lord,
　and my ardent prayer is that even in my dying,
like the sun—like Gideon too—
　I might go in the strength that I have,
to fight your battles and run your race,
　in the power that only you can provide.
Then, like Moses, maybe the day will come,
　when I have spent my life at your pleasure,
　　to find myself on the doorstep of your Presence.
Will you see in my eyes
　a light that does not fade
　and a strength that is not gone?
Where, O Lord, will I find that strength,
　but in the hands that formed the heavens?
Where will I obtain the fuel for never-ending fire,
　if not in the One who powers the sun?
To love you, Lord, with all my heart,
　and all my soul, and all my strength,
I must be more than I am—
　I must be part of you, and you, all of me.
One more time, Lord, I pray,
　listen to man—
　　to the one who kneels before you now.
Stop the sun if you must,
　but be my strength,
　　and fight with me to your glorious end!

†Joshua 10:1-15

† 2 Timothy 1:6-7

Questions for Reflection and Prayer:

1. What does it mean to love the Lord with all your heart, and all your soul, and all your strength? Is this even possible? And if so, how? Are there any biblical examples—other than Christ—of men who obeyed this command? What did their lives look like (see 2 Kings 22-23; 2 Chronicles 34-35)?

2. Christianity makes the bold claim that one can only be confident about his or her true existence precisely when one ceases to exist. How is that possible? Philosopher Paul Tillich says the following concerning this paradox:

> For the courage of confidence is not rooted in confidence about oneself. The Reformation pronounces the opposite: one can become confident about one's existence only after ceasing to base one's confidence on oneself...It [the courage of confidence] is based on God and solely on God, who is experienced in a unique and personal encounter.

As Tillich notes, claiming one's existence with confidence—the "courage to be"—requires a personal encounter with God, the source of all being. Have you had your encounter?

3. David says in Psalm 19, "The heavens declare the glory of God; the skies proclaim the work of His hands." In the story from Joshua, the heavens declare God's glory in a special way. But even if the sun does not stand still, is our small star any less marvelous? Take a moment to contemplate the sun and consider the glory of the God who made it.

References
Dt 6:5; 34:7; Jdg 6:14; Ps 18:1; 59:17; 73:26; Isa 45:24; 2 Tim 1:6-7

Diving Deeper:

1. J.D. Eubanks, MD, "The Greatest Commandment" in *More of Him, Less of Me* (Dawn Treader, LLC, 2018), 92.
2. Paul Tillich, *The Courage To Be* (New Haven, CT: Yale University Press, 2014, 150.

The Twenty-sixth Hour

Psalm 38:11-12—My friends and companions avoid me
because of my wounds;
my neighbors stay far away.
Those who seek my life set their traps,
those who would harm me talk of my ruin;
all day long they plot deception.

To pitch my tent with you, O Lord,
and to follow where you lead,
sometimes brings me to no man's land.
For true faithfulness demands solitary places,
and the man of God, faithful to the will of God,
will find that stretch of narrow road
where companions are sparse and encouragement thin.
To each one you whisper your will;
and though we look for you in wind, earthquake and fire,
your voice often chooses a gentle step.
How will I hear you softly treading
amidst the constant trample of feet?
This I have learned from you—
though three in one, and always One triune,
you sought the One in solitary places.
So in solitude I seek the three-cornered fortress;
for unless inside those walls, I am not with you, Lord.
Untruth lives in the raucous crowd;[8]
and where there are many tents,
there are many places to hide.
For few who say they desire you, God, really do;
and to hold your cup is not to drink it down.
Even the prophet is rejected in his hometown;
and some with whom I have shared sweet fellowship
have proved turncoats or wanderers.
Familiarity may bring the twin pains
of desertion and disappointment;

---

[8] Søren Kierkegaard, "That Individual," in *Existentialism from Dostoevsky to Sartre*, ed. Walter Kaufmann (New York: Plume, 1975), 94-5.

89

but the darkness carries the hunters.
For the true battle is not against flesh and blood,
  but those shadowed principalities;
and the real war is always the unseen one,
  waged by a skillful scheming that despises
    the standard you, Lord, have called me to carry.
With subtle craft the demons lay their traps,
  even as their dark riders
    pursue me with foaming tenacity.
I am a man—like you, Jesus—hunted by hate;
  when they sling their arrows, they aim for you in me.
So we are chased into the landscape of liminality,
  that barren strip between animus and rejection,
bounded by the enemies who hotly pursue
  and the companions who quietly walk away.
It is a place that you, my Lord, know well,
  situated between the shoulders
of the confused kiss that betrays,
  and the prideful whip that scourges.
Because this land rejected you, it holds me a stranger,
  exiled to a world that waits for your return.
Gershom may as well be my name,
  for I too am a child of the journey,
born into a desert sojourn
  that seeks the fulfillment of God's promise.
But though arid country stretches before me,
  endless in its reach, bleak in its near predictions,
I comfort in the cloud that leads by day,
  and the blazing pillar that beacons in the night.
And though an unseen army pursues me,
  and the men alongside may rise up against me,
I give you thanks for this solitary place,
  peopled by the few true companions you bring
    and Heaven's immovable tenancy.
For you alone will never leave me, nor forsake me;
  your Presence will be my constant companion.
Through the tears I shed for the falling,
    I will rejoice;
through the sweat that runs from my hunting,
    I will give thanks.
For a man of many companions may come to ruin,
  but there is a Friend who sticks closer than a brother,
    and He is the lover of my soul.

Selected Readings for Further Study

† 1 Kings 19:9-18

† Ephesians 6:10-20

Questions for Reflection and Prayer:

1. Danish philosopher Søren Kierkegaard speaks of the crowd as the "untruth." What does he mean? Kierkegaard says, "a crowd in its very concept is the untruth, by reason of the fact that it renders the individual completely impenitent and irresponsible, or at least weakens his sense of responsibility by reducing it to a fraction." How can the individual man hide from himself in the crowd? Spiritually, how can that be dangerous? What are the potential implications for eternity?

2. Why does solitude matter to our spiritual lives? Jesus often sought solitary places to be with the Father. Do you? And if not, how can you begin to make those places a priority in your life?

3. The Dark Riders are one of the most haunting images emerging from Tolkien's *The Fellowship of the Ring*. As Tolkien describes them, "they appeared to have cast aside their hoods and black cloaks, and they were robed in white and grey. Swords were naked in their pale hands; helms were on their heads. Their cold eyes glittered, and they called to him [Frodo] with fell voices." Tolkien's description evokes the Apostle Paul's reminder to the Ephesians: "For our struggle is not against flesh and blood, but against the rulers, against the authorities, against the powers of this dark world and against the spiritual forces of evil in the heavenly realms"(Eph 6:12)? Can you feel that war waging against you even now?

References
        Ex 2:22; 1 Kings 19:9-18; Ps 55:12-14; 119:19; Pr 18:24; Lk 4:24;
        Jn 15:18; 17:16; Heb 11:13; Rev 8:35-39

Diving Deeper:

1. J.D. Eubanks, MD, "Lonely Places, I." in *More of Him, Less of Me* (Dawn Treader, LLC, 2018), 44.
2. J.D. Eubanks, MD, "The Stranger" in *More of Him, Less of Me* (Dawn Treader, LLC, 2018), 370.
3. Søren Kierkegaard, "That Individual," in *Existentialism from Dostoevsky to Sartre*, ed. Walter Kaufmann (New York: Plume, 1975), 94-5.
4. J.R.R. Tolkien, *The Fellowship of the Ring* (Boston: Houghton Mifflin, 1987), 226.

The Twenty-seventh Hour

Psalm 38:13-14—I am like a deaf man, who cannot hear,
like a mute, who cannot open his mouth.
I have become like a man who does not hear,
whose mouth can offer no reply.

Like solitary places, O Lord,

the soul needs silence.
For without the hush, the roots are too shallow,
the weeds are too thick,
and the ground too parched—
nothing grows.
In the silence one finds the Source,
and kneeling there,
in the quiet that swallows desperation,
he may drink deeply from the headwaters.
But your greatness, God, gushes forth,
as it pushes out beyond mere silence;
and to never journey downstream
amidst rapids that threaten as they deafen,
would be to risk a life without beauty
in a vacuum devoid of you.
For the blind will say, sound and touch
give more sight than sight itself.
Who knows but you, O Lord?
But this much is true—
your greatness only gathers strength
as it flows down
into your teeming, squawking flatlands—
the fullness of you.
For you are in the noise as much as the silence;
and your Presence fills the bustling valley,
as much as the lonely crags.
You play out in innumerable faces,
some seen, some heard—
the infant's smile, and a child's laughter;
falling tresses of mahogany hair;
the warbler's song and a dragonfly's wings.

Through beauty you speak to us
  in a language universal and personal,
    large as the cosmos, small as the atom.
In one instance, an utterance undeniable;
  in another, subject
    to the eye of your beholder:
A voice of sight, sound, smell and taste,
  that declares you all the same—
    loud as a trumpet, soft as a kiss.
Who can stand deaf before these overtures?
  Who can remain silent before your beauty?
By what name shall we call that demon
  who denies the Lord in His radiant glory?
Does the symphony not have a composer?
  What sculpture emerges from the air?
Is the earth not full of your music, Lord,
  and the globe a great gallery
    for all your artistry?
Once there was boy, deaf and mute,
  gripped by an inner demon,
who fell before you in a fit of rage,
  convulsing before your power.
But with a prayerful word, Lord,
  you drove that dark spirit out;
and the boy, though many took as dead,
  rose again by your hand—
for as you said, "*Everything is possible
  for him who believes.*"
Who is the boy resurrected, but me,
  once deaf and mute before you?
Who is that shrieking spirit
  who bound me from your beauty,
    a self, possessed of self?
But for your grace, O Lord,
  I am the demon as much as the boy.
Foaming at the mouth, gnashing my teeth,
  rigid against your touch—
    deaf and mute before you, Lord,
until…your word set me free,
  and your hand raised me up—
    beautiful before Beauty.
O Lord, *I do believe; help me overcome my unbelief!*

Selected Readings for Further Study

† Isaiah 29:18-21

† Mark 9:14-32

Questions for Reflection and Prayer:

1. Solomon says, "There is a time for everything" (Ecc 3:1). Silence is no exception. Akin to solitary places, there must also be mandatory times for the space of silence. Sometimes solitary places and silent spaces even go hand in hand. But they needn't always. Why are these moments of silence so important to our spiritual lives? Why did Jesus seek them out? Have you made them a regular part of your life?

2. Forgetting all other proofs for God, the beauty of creation points us to the Creator. And this beauty comes to *all* our senses. For as the blind and deaf, Helen Keller, says, "The keenness of our vision depends not on how much we can see, but on how much we feel. Nor yet does mere knowledge create beauty. Nature sings her most exquisite songs to those who love her." Have you allowed your senses to take in the beauty of God's world in a way that draws your spirit to Him? Can you see, feel, smell, and hear His power, glory and love in everything around you?

3. Have you had—or perhaps you still do—an inner demon that throws you into fits of rage before the King? If you believe, you can be freed. Do you believe?

References
> Ex 4:11; Isa 29:18-21; Mk 7:31-34; 9:14-32.

Diving Deeper:

1. J.D. Eubanks, MD, "Different Forms, Same God" in *More of Him, Less of Me* (Dawn Treader, LLC, 2018), 76.
2. J.D. Eubanks, MD, "Tracks" in *Twelve Stones: Apologetics for an Age of Relativism* (Dawn Treader, LLC, 2022), 33-45.
3. Helen Keller, *The World I Live In & Optimism* (Garden City, NY: Dover Publications, 2009), 41.

The Twenty-eighth Hour

Psalm 38:15—I wait for you, O Lord;
you will answer, O Lord my God.

Why, O Lord, have you woven
      so much waiting
   into the tapestry of your world?
Before our first breath,
   we wait in the water of the womb.
Then bursting forth with a scream,
   we enter a life
      full of pregnant moments—
some short, some long,
   but always a tiring struggle
      between moment and man.
In the pain of sleepless nights,
   we wait with eager expectation
      for the coming of dawn.
Amidst the ceaseless labors of day,
   we yearn for the rest of night.
Then it begins again—
   the sun that rises and sets and rises again.
Is all this work of waiting truly meaningless?
   Is there no purpose
      to this labor under the sun?
Before diligent hands, the farmer's harvest waits
   for a rain that may never come.
The beloved longs for the return
   of her long lost lover,
even as the wronged queues her expectations
   for an unlikely apology.
Do they wait in vain?
   Can their fulfillment be assured?
Nature, too, is full of your waiting—
   the buried bulbs panting for spring;
   the lion lying low in the tall grass;
      and the hawk perched on a limb, watching—

95

waiting for the perfect moment
  to leap into action.
No doubt, this pounce is part of your plan, God—
  for its readiness speaks of timing, timing of promise,
    and promise of confident expectation.
To leap, one must possess necessity:
  a desperate despair or a determined hope.
Before you leapt into action, Lord,
  you waited in a carpenter's shop,
while the necessity of your sacrifice
  patiently queued in wood shavings.
Before you turned water into wine,
  the hands that created the universe
    waited in the work of tables and chairs.
You waited for the odor of Lazarus,
  before you raised him from the dead.
And you waited to return to Zion,
  until, like the seed in warming soil,
    you knew your time had come.
You waited; and you still wait—
    so must we.
Like the virgins tending our lamps,
  always ready to open the door to your knock—
waiting and watching with our whole being,
  in a hope that exceeds mere aspiration.
For since the first dawn,
  no eye has seen, no ear has heard
of any God besides you, Lord,
  who acts on behalf of those who wait for Him.
So blessed are those who wait for you—
  for the strength you provide for today,
    and the hope you promise for tomorrow.
Blessed are those days of hard service
  that wait for your renewal.
For your coming is coming, Lord,
  and all creation builds
    an altar to your hastening return.
While we wait for this blessed hope,
  give us grace to live in this present age.
May we find in our waiting
  the freeing freedom of trusting,
as we mount up on the wings of eagles
  and soar toward your coming promise.

Selected Readings for Further Study

† Isaiah 64:1-4

† Matthew 25:1-13

Questions for Reflection and Prayer:

1. Oswald Chambers says, "If our hopes seem to be experiencing disappointment right now, it simply means that they are being purified. Every hope or dream of the human mind will be fulfilled if it is noble and of God. But one of the greatest stresses in life is the stress of waiting for God."
What have you had to painstakingly wait for in your life? What did you learn about yourself in the process of waiting? What did you learn about God?

2. God Himself is a God who waits. Why is that important? Does the prolonged latency of His promise fulfillment mean the waiting is in vain? What did a servant like Abraham do in his waiting? Did he give up? Did he lose faith?

3. Is our waiting on God passive or active? In looking at the parable of the ten virgins, theologian Kenneth Bailey suggests the parable points out "Jesus' *disappointment at the lack of readiness* to receive the kingdom when it arrives. In his ministry, Jesus inaugurated the kingdom of God and was disappointed that many around him, who had been waiting for the revelation of that kingdom, were not prepared for it when it arrived." Are you prepared? What does Jesus want us to learn from the virgins tending their lamps? How should we wait for Him?

References
Job 14:14; Ps 33:20; 130:5; Ecc 3:2-3; Isa 30:18; 64:1-4; La 3:24; Hos 12:6; Mic 7:7; Mt 25:1-13; Titus 2:11-14;

Diving Deeper:

1. J.D. Eubanks, MD, "Wait, Wait, Wait…Go" in *More of Him, Less of Me* (Dawn Treader, LLC, 2018), 186.
2. Oswald Chamber, *My Utmost for His Highest* (Grand Rapids, MI: Discovery House Publishers, 1992), February 22.
3. Kenneth E. Bailey, *Jesus Through Middle Eastern Eyes* (Downers Grove, IL: InterVarsity Press, 2008), 275.

The Twenty-ninth Hour

Psalm 38:16-17—For I said, "Do not let them gloat
or exalt themselves over me
when my foot slips."
For I am about to fall,
and my pain is ever with me.

O Lord, your way is a rough road,

littered with stones to make us stumble
and a Rock that makes us fall.
But why do we fear to fall,
when the Rock that fells us
redeems us?
Why do we choose the broad, smooth path,
when the stones that make us stumble
lead us to the Truth?
No doubt, the hell-bound bandits
who line the King's highway
are partly to blame;
lurking in the shadows, they shoot their arrows,
and stand over me in a transient triumph.
Who wants to live his life
with a target on his back,
never sure when the darkness will strike?
Who chooses to be an enemy
of the country he must pass through,
knowing he will be hated and hunted?
But the pain of your path, O God,
is also part of our parting.
For those stones over which we stumble
bruise our bodies and our souls,
to remind us we are mortal gods
who cannot make it on our own.
Far easier to live in a lie
that knows no near impediments;
far sweeter to grab what we want,
when we want it,
as we build idols to ourselves.

But what happens, Lord,
    when we treat you with contempt—
when we try to drag your Presence
    before the gods we have made?
For when the sun rose in Ashdod,
        wasn't the statue of Dagon
            fallen on its face before you?
And though human hands raised it anew,
    you, O Lord, forced it to bow again,
        breaking insolence to pieces.
Your Presence was too much for them,
    and the Philistines sent you away—
        some of us have too.
Forgive us, Father, for the monuments
    we build to ourselves,
and those days we wish your power
    was loaded on an ox-driven cart,
        headed someplace else.
Thank you for the force that pulls me down,
    for the stones that make me stumble,
        and the Rock that makes me fall.
For in falling, your hand may lift me up;
    in stumbling, your arm supports me.
For the Lord upholds those who fall before Him,
    and His hand raises all who are bowed down.
And though the righteous man falls
    seven times,
        seven times, he rises again.
Not a sparrow falls apart from your will, O God.
    How much more are your eyes upon me?
So when I fall, let it be towards you, Lord;
    when I pitch my tent,
        may I make the Most High my dwelling.
Then your angels will surround me;
    they will guard me and protect me;
    they will lift me up with their hands—
until one day, I see you face to face,
    and falling down before you,
I throw my crown at the feet
    of the only King
        whose countenance is capable
    of keeping my heart singing.

99

Selected Readings for Further Study

† 1 Samuel 5:1-12

† Romans 9:30-33

Questions for Reflection and Prayer:

1. Stumbling is part of walking God's narrow road. Though it hurts to stub our toes, how does that pain change us? We can grow bitter and disillusioned, or wiser and more dependent on the Guide leading us. Which option are you choosing?

2. The Philistine god, Dagon, could not stand before the ark of the Lord's Presence. Have you built an idol that you are trying to prop up before the Presence of God? Will it not, like Dagon, fall face down before the King? Will it elude death?

   Many attempt to avoid ultimate questions like death by living a lie. But as Tolstoy admits in his autobiographical, *A Confession*, sooner or later all lies meet existential truth:

> The old delusive joys of life, which used to assuage my terror of the dragon, no longer deceived me. You could say to me as often as you liked, "You can't understand the meaning of life—don't think, live!" I couldn't do that because I had done it for too long before. Now I couldn't fail to see day and night hurrying on and leading me to death. I saw only that, because that alone was the truth. All the rest was a lie.

Faced with truth, Tolstoy finally found his way out of his lie. Have you?

3. As Solomon reminds us, when the righteous fall, they will rise again. But the wicked will one day fall, never to rise (Pr 24:16). Why does the "end zone" perspective matter for every fall in-between?

References
   1 Sam 5:1-12; 2 Sam 24:14; Ps 37:24; 91:9-12; 145:14; Pr 24:16; Mt 10:29; Ro 9:30-33; Rev 4:10

Diving Deeper:

1. J.D. Eubanks, MD, "The Redeemed Stumbler" in *More of Him, Less of Me* (Dawn Treader, LLC, 2018), 182.
2. J.D. Eubanks, MD, "Denouement" in *Twelve Stones: Apologetics for an Age of Relativism* (Dawn Treader, LLC, 2022), 183-185.
3. Leo Tolstoy, *A Confession* (Joseph Simon Publisher, 1982), 102.

The Thirtieth Hour

Psalm 38:18—I confess my iniquity;
　　　　I am troubled by my sin.

Almighty God, I am troubled by my sin,
　by the deep down darkness within.
But from where does this unrest come?
　Why does iniquity bother me?
If the world is, as they say it is,
　without God,
　　why do I yearn for justice?
For justice speaks of poles—
　north and south, up and down,
　　black and white, right and wrong.
Justice cannot live in a gray world;
　and where there is light,
　　there will be lines.
When push comes to shove,
　justice stands or falls on absolutes—
　　for where everything goes, nothing matters.
But who will drop these plumb lines?
　For if they do not fall from Heaven,
　　they will never be straight.
The shoddy structures we build
　with their crooked alternatives,
　　will always be crooked.
　　　　~
Iniquity or inequity?
　Do they not share a common birth?
For they emerge from a breach of justice
　as fraternal twins, one grasping the heel of the other—
　　separate, but rarely inseparable.
Iniquity is the son I know all too well,
　for he comes from my callous heart.
He is the villainy I came with,
　and the selfishness that never ceases
　　to go grabbing from you, God.

101

Iniquity is the inner demon
  that dies a lingering death.
It is the snake without a head,
  still thrashing in the throes of dying.
But inequity is the injustice outside,
  the lack of level
    in the world beyond my inner temple.
Sometimes I feel his touch as well;
  but most often he marches with causes—
some good, some bad.
Sometimes pleading, sometimes screaming,
  inequity rails against unfairness and favoritism.
And though inequity may find its moral champion,
  equally it may become the tool
    of iniquitous hands.
For the world screams for justice,
  and yet no man truly wants justice
    when justice comes for him.
                    ~
You, O Lord, are the God of Justice,
  and your coming Son will bring His scales.
Iniquity will be weighed;
  inequity will be banished.
Those who seek to throw down Heaven
  and level the world with fickle consensus,
will be judged by the One they judged,
  as the White Throne's ruling
    comes smashing down upon them.
But those who call upon your Name, Lord,
  will realize your great compassion;
and the One who bore their iniquities
  will forever tread their sins underfoot,
    as He hurls them with finality
    into the depths of the vanishing sea.
Iniquity be warned, your last breath is coming.
  Inequity be glad, for you shall be healed.
Let him who does wrong continue to do wrong;
  let him who is vile continue to be vile;
let him who does right continue to do right;
  let him who is holy continue to be holy.
"Behold, I am coming soon!
  My reward is with me, and I will give to everyone
    according to what he has done."

Selected Readings for Further Study

† Genesis 25:19-34

† Revelation 22:7-21

<u>Questions for Reflection and Prayer:</u>

1. The German philosopher, Immanuel Kant, has a tombstone near the cathedral of Kaliningrad that contains this quote from his *Critique of Practical Reason*: "Two things fill the mind with ever new and increasing admiration and awe, the more often and steadily we reflect upon them: the starry heavens above me and the moral law within me." What is Kant saying here? Does the moral law within—that transcends centuries, races, and cultures—point to a Law-giver?

2. We live in a world crazed with inequality agendas. How will those campaigns fare without considering the iniquity within? What is the only way to heal the inequalities of our world? Can it be done through a political solution? Charles Taylor says:

> To come together on a mutual recognition of difference—that is, of the equal value of different identities—requires that we share more than a belief in this principle; we have to share also some standards of value on which identities concerned check out to be equal....We can pay lip-service to equal recognition, but we won't really share an understanding of equality unless we share something more. Recognizing this difference...requires a horizon of significance, in this case a shared one.

When a culture throws out the sacred, what is the "horizon of significance"?

3. The Judgement of the Great White Throne will judge iniquity. For Christians, this is good news! For though they have iniquity in their hearts, Christ will see only His blood covering those hearts. Have you chosen to be covered in that blood?

References
  Ge 25:19-34; Ps 73:7; Isa 53:5, 11; Mic 7:19; Rev 22:7-21

<u>Diving Deeper:</u>

1. J.D. Eubanks, MD, "Examine Yourself" in *More of Him, Less of Me* (Dawn Treader, LLC, 2018), 340.
 2. Charles Taylor, *The Ethics of Authenticity* (Cambridge, MA: Harvard University Press, 1991), 52.

103

The Thirty-first Hour

Psalm 38:19-20—Many are those who are my vigorous enemies;
those who hate me without reason are numerous.
Those who repay my good with evil
slander me when I pursue what is good.

W hy, O Lord, must my lot
   be the ruined wall,
this rubble of a rebellion
   you could no longer tolerate?
The reek of our sin reached Heaven,
   wafting on the wind,
until even you, Lord, long of nose,
   could no longer stand the stench.
We brought the walls down around us,
   and our sin alone
      set your city aflame.
         ~
Here I am, Almighty God,
   with a difficult leg to run.
For mine is not the gilded beauty
   of Solomon's Temple,
but the charred rock of chastening
   and the endless work of rebuilding.
Mine is not the time of plenty and peace;
   for though the nations lie quiet,
      the enemy rises within
      to spoil your plenty.
Mine is a true labor of love,
   bathed in sweat and tears,
      sword at my side—
a task too big for my hands,
   and a work too heavy for my heart.
My enemies know it too,
   circling like laughing jackals
   as they hurl their insults at God and man.
With the dagger-jabs of lies,
   my foes try to frustrate your work, O Lord.

They mock me in fear of you;
  they reach for the low-hanging fruit.
For I am only a section of the wall;
  but you, O God, are the power within.
And if I fail, they hope for a hole
  through which they can still run.
But have they forgotten
  what leveled these stones—
how we mocked your messengers,
  despised your words,
    and scoffed at your prophets,
until your wrath was aroused
  and no remedy remained?
And do they not know,
  that even if I do fall,
  you are more than the God of gaps—
you are the One who can fill their abyss;
  and that once decided,
    your work cannot be stopped.
In my earthen vessel, let this glory reside;
  may your all-surpassing power
    pour out from me.
Now strengthen my hands, O God, I pray;
  give me the courage to do your work,
    one stone at a time.

              ~

But if I may be so bold, O Lord,
  one thing further I ask.
Give me not only the strength for your work,
  but also the heart to see it through.
For though every ounce of who I am
  longs to turn my enemies' insults
    back upon their heads,
grant that I may be more than I am—
  to bless those who persecute me,
    and pray for those who speak evil against me—
      to be perfect, as you are perfect.
For as it is, revenge I can fathom,
  but grace bends my brain.
Reward I can calculate,
  but your love defies arithmetic.
For your love saw the enemy in me,
  and your grace still chose to set me free.

Selected Readings for Further Study

† Nehemiah 4:1-21

† Matthew 5:10-12; 43-48

Questions for Reflection and Prayer:

1. In the Book of Nehemiah, the enemies of Israel mock and ridicule the work of rebuilding the wall around Jerusalem. What were they trying to accomplish and why? When people in your life ridicule or persecute you for doing God's work, can you—like the early disciples in Acts (5:17-42)—learn to give thanks?

2. Blaise Pascal says, "...the infinite abyss can only be filled by an infinite and immutable object, that is to say, only by God Himself." Rather than filling the abyss with God, some attempt to pack it with other things; some choose to deny the abyss altogether. In this denial, the latter group—like the scientific, New Atheists—may even go on the offensive against God and His people. As Richard Dawkins says, "you will lead a better, fuller life if you bet on his [God's] not existing, than if you bet on his existing and therefore squander your precious time on worshipping him, sacrificing to him, fighting and dying for him, etc." Have you, like Nehemiah and his workers, been on the receiving end of this venomous assault? What can you learn from the response of Nehemiah and his workers that might be helpful for your life?

3. Revenging wrong committed against us is a natural inclination. Forgiveness and blessing those who curse us, on the other hand, is a supernatural response. Christ calls us to the latter. Have you made a habit of asking for the Spirit's assistance to love your enemies?

References
2 Ch 36:16; Neh 4:1-21; Mt 5:10-12; 43-48; Acts 5:17-42; 2 Cor 4:7-9

Diving Deeper:

1. J.D. Eubanks, MD, "Strengthen My Hands" in *More of Him, Less of Me* (Dawn Treader, LLC, 2018), 192.
2. Blaise Pascal, *Pensées* (New York: The Modern Library, 1941), 135.
3. John C. Lennox, *Gunning for God: Why the New Atheists are Missing the Target* (Oxford, England: Lion, 2011).
4. Richard Dawkins, *The God Delusion* (New York: Mariner Books, 2008), 131-132.

106

The Thirty-second Hour

Psalm 38:21-22—O Lord, do not forsake me;
be not far from me, O God.
Come quickly to help me,
O Lord, my Savior.

Y ou, O God, are the Lord of Paradox,

and to know you is to wrestle
with your contrarian complexities.
For your truth is more than odd,
and because it is,
some part of us knows it is true.
For life is seldom neat and tidy,
and any truth making sense of our mess,
must at once be starkly simple
and terribly complicated;
smooth as a baby's cheek,
but prickly as a pear in full bloom.
It must be a binding yoke of ironies,
full of nothing but seeming absurdities,
which make no sense of the absurd,
until one embraces absurdity—
then perforce, the odd truths
become the only obvious Truth,
and everything else, a vanishing vapor.
For if you want to save your life,
you must lose it;
if you desire to become the greatest,
you must deign to be the least;
if you will to be strong,
you cannot be but weak;
if you aspire to be exalted,
you must consider stooping;
and if you dare to grasp wisdom,
you must venture to become a fool.

~

What then shall we say for your Presence?
Does your proximity also bow
to your paradigm of paradox?

107

For have you not said,
  "*Never will I leave you,*
    never will I forsake you"?
And did you not promise,
  "*I am with you always,*
    to the very end of the age"?
But in this moment, I confess, Lord,
  I do not feel your nearness,
    much less see your face.
And your words to your slow companions
  seem, in this hour, a cold comfort—
"It is for your good that I am going away.
  Unless I go away, the Counselor will not come;
    but if I go, I will send him to you."
You had to go to come?
  You had to leave our presence,
    to make your Presence omnipresent in us?
In departing, did you permanently arrive?
  In your goodbye, did you forever say, "Hello"?

              ~

Still, there is no seasoned saint
  who doesn't long to look on your face;
and though you are here with us, in us,
  at times, the distance seems too great.
For the paradox of proximity lies in this:
  that those who know you best,
  and long for you most,
sometimes receive the trust of your withdrawal—
  the deep love of your step back,
    to watch—for a moment—as we walk alone.
Job in Uz and Christ on Golgatha,
  both felt your release.
  But did your love leave them?
And Hezekiah's faithfulness earned your distance,
  as you left him to test him,
    and to know everything that was in his heart.
For you, O God, are the Lord of Paradox;
  and those who think themselves nearest,
    are sometimes most far;
and the seemingly far are,
  at times, nearest to your heart.

Selected Readings for Further Study

† 2 Kings 18:1-7; 2 Chronicles 32:24-31

† John 16:5-16

Questions for Reflection and Prayer:

1. Christianity is a faith of paradoxes. G. K. Chesterton says, "Not merely that it [Christianity] deduces logical truths, but that when it suddenly becomes illogical, it has found, so to speak, an illogical truth." And yet, the "illogical" truth is still true. What biblical paradox means most to you? Which "illogical" truth is the hardest pill for you to swallow?

2. Christian mystic, John van Ruysbroeck, once said, "We come from God and we are in exile; and it is because our potency of affection tends toward God that we are aware of this state of exile." Why do those who know God best sometimes struggle most with a sense of their distance from Him? In the Messianic Psalm 22 (quoted by Christ on the cross) David repeatedly says to God, "Do not be far from me…"(v. 11). How could David, the man after God's own heart, much less Jesus, the Son of God, feel far from God?

3. Can God's momentary distance be a sign of His deepest love and affection? Why?

References
        2 Ki 18:1-7; 2 Ch 32:24-31; Mt 16:25; 19:30; 23:12; 20:26-27; 28:20;
        1 Cor 3:18; 2 Cor 12:10

Diving Deeper:

1. J.D. Eubanks, MD, "Left Him to Test Him" in *More of Him, Less of Me* (Dawn Treader, LLC, 2018), 96.
2. J.D. Eubanks, MD, "Exile and the Kingdom" in *Twelve Stones: Apologetics for an Age of Relativism* (Dawn Treader, LLC, 2022), 9-32.
3. G.K. Chesterton, *Orthodoxy* (Peabody, MA: Hendrickson Publishers Marketing, LLC, 2006), 78.

IV.

Psalm 51

A psalm of David. When the prophet Nathan
came to him after David had committed adultery
with Bathsheba.

Have mercy on me, O God,
  according to your unfailing love;
according to your great compassion
  blot out my transgressions.
Wash away all my iniquity
  and cleanse me from my sin.
For I know my transgressions,
  and my sin is always before me.
Against you, you only, have I sinned
  and done what is evil in your sight,
so that you are proved right when you speak
  and justified when you judge.
Surely I was sinful from birth,
  sinful from the time my mother conceived me.
Surely you desire truth in the inner parts;
  you teach me wisdom in the inmost place.
Cleanse me with hyssop and I will be clean;
  wash me, and I will be whiter than snow.
Let me hear joy and gladness;
  let the bones you have crushed rejoice.
Hide your face from my sins
  and blot out all my iniquity.
Create in me a clean heart, O God,
  and renew a steadfast spirit within me.
Do not cast me from your Presence
  or take your Holy Spirit from me.

111

Restore to me the joy of your salvation
   and grant me a willing spirit to sustain me.
Then I will teach transgressors your ways,
   and sinners will turn back to you.
Save me from bloodguilt, O God,
   the God who saves me,
   and my tongue will sing of your righteousness.
O Lord, open my lips,
   and my mouth will declare your praise.
You do not delight in sacrifice, or I would bring it;
   you do not take pleasure in burnt offerings.
The sacrifices of God are a broken spirit;
   a broken and contrite heart,
   O God, you will not despise.
In your good pleasure make Zion prosper;
   build up the walls of Jerusalem.
Then there will be righteous sacrifices,
   whole burnt offerings to delight you;
   then bulls will be offered on your altar.

The Thirty-third Hour

Psalm 51:1-2—Have mercy on me, O God,
according to your unfailing love;
according to your great compassion
blot out my transgressions.

Mercy is meaningless, O God,

until a man is thrown overboard
into the rage of the unforgiving sea.
But even then, when the waves threaten
to crush him,
he might still resist rescue.
For as long as there is any plank
his arms can cling to,
any shore he thinks he can swim towards,
he will not reach out to you.
~
I am never far from Jonah;
and the man who ran from you, O Lord,
still, at times, runs in me.
But even Jonah knew the hungry sea
would not calm without a sacrifice.
For between the golden wings of cherubim
there was still a smoky sea,
where your rage against sin only quieted
with the blood of bulls.
Atonement is never a joke,
and forgiveness never without blood.
Yet on a ship headed for Tarshish,
your mercy began to move in man
as Jonah was thrown into the depths.
Three days and three nights—
a descent to presage
the descent to end all descents.
For no sign shall be shown
but the sign of Jonah,
to mark mercy's greatest act.
~

113

You, O Lord, are the giver of all mercy,
the High Priest who sacrificed Himself,
once for all.
You, Jesus, are the last Adam,
the life-giving Spirit
whose blood forever stills
the wrath of your raging sea.
For at just the right time,
when we were still powerless,
flailing in turbulent depths,
you died for the ungodly—
you bled for rebels like me.

~

Compassion breathes with love;
mercy is the fruit of compassion.
Because of your great love for us, O God—
because you are rich in mercy—
we have been made alive with Christ,
even when we were drowning in our sins.
For the Son of God is the great High Priest,
who has gone through the heavens
with mercy on His mind.
Christ is the Priest of priests,
who knows all our temptations
and sympathizes with our all weaknesses—
and yet, was without sin.

~

I am a sinner before you, Perfect Priest;
I am a surly prophet on the run,
testing your raging sea.
Yet in love, you took on my flesh;
you tossed yourself into the angry depths.
With a great gulp, the fathoms were satisfied;
swallowing my rebellion,
the peace of God fell upon the waters.
Now before me I look upon a sea of glass;
the calm of confidence in the eye of the storm
unfurls before your throne, O Lord.
And though the devil's sirens still sing,
there is a miracle in me—
in the escort of your unfailing love,
I boldly advance
toward a throne gilded in grace.

114

<u>Selected Readings for Further Study</u>

† Exodus 25:19-22; Jonah 1-2

† Hebrews 9:11-28

<u>Questions for Reflection and Prayer:</u>

1. C.S. Lewis says, "The human spirit will not even begin to try to surrender self-will as long as all seems to be well with it.....While what we call 'our own life' remains agreeable we will not surrender it to Him." What did it take for Jonah to surrender? What did it (will it?) take for you?

2. Jonah was a prophet well familiar with the sacrifices necessary for the atonement of sin under the first covenant. When his life is put up for sacrifice, what happens? How does this event foreshadow Christ's sacrifice? What is the "Sign of Jonah" Christ alludes to (Mt 16:4)?

3. The Hebrew word, *kapporeth*, speaks of the ransom associated with the mercy seat of God. The writer of Hebrews tells us Christ became that ransom to set us free from the sins committed under the first covenant (9:15). What does it mean that Christ became a "ransom" for you? How does Christ's ransom give us confidence before the throne of God? Are you resting in that *chesed* ("mercy," as in goodness or kindness)?

References
> Ex 25:19-22; Lev 16; Mt 16:4; Ro 5:6-11; 1 Cor 15:45; Eph 2:4-5; Heb 4:16; 9:11-28

<u>Diving Deeper:</u>

1. J.D. Eubanks, MD, "The Jonah Within" in *More of Him, Less of Me* (Dawn Treader, LLC, 2018), 32.
2. C.S. Lewis, *The Problem of Pain* (New York: HarperCollins, 1996), 90, 94.

🐋

115

The Thirty-fourth Hour

Psalm 51:3-4—For I know my transgressions,
and my sin is always before me.
Against you [Lord], you only, have I sinned
and done what is evil in your sight,
so that you are proved right when you speak
and justified when you judge.

Where is the man, O God,

whose transgressions elude him,
who finds himself forever faultless,
a perfect sphere spinning
in a frictionless universe?
To be a man is to wobble;
and to be an honest man
is to know why.
For since the bitter juice
of the fateful fruit,
conscience cannot forever lie,
save in the man who is no longer man,
but a demon dancing the devil's jig.
But even the devil knows his wrong;
and the darkness will smile with pride
to admit its fault.
For simply knowing one's sin
does not make the saint;
and confession only prepares the way
for the softened heart or the hardened will
to follow to its desired end.

~

So where will my sin settle, O Lord—
before my sight or behind my back?
Will it be an anchor I drag
in the secret depths—
a leaden weight I know well,
but a burden I refuse to acknowledge?
Or will my guilt stand like the mountain it is,
immovable and unscalable,
by anyone but you?

116

But then I remember your promise,
  which you declared as true—
that if anyone says to this mountain,
  "Go, throw yourself into the sea,"
and does not doubt, but believes—
  even that mountain—my mountain too—
    may go hurtling into the deep.

~

Faith is the force that frees;
  grace is the gift to go on living.
For who can stand
  before the Judge he has wronged?
Who can hope for a hung jury,
  in jury of One?
I am a man on trial, full of fault,
  finding no one else for the fall.
My failures fail you, O God,
  when they fail no other,
    when they fail all.
Where the world sees nothing,
  your gaze pierces through.
When the kiss comes as a guilty cover,
  you are proved right when you speak,
    and justified when you judge.
But sin exposed is not without hope,
  and transgressions confessed
    can be Love's greatest ministers.
For what if the well of experience
  is not plugged,
and my repentance were to pour forth
  your purified spring?
Can the suffering not drink
  of what you have done in me, O Lord?
May you not make of fits, fuss and failures,
  a sweet song of your redeeming love?
For blessed is the man of faith;
  he believes what he cannot see.
Blessed is the lover in us all, O Lord,
  the man who loves as you love me—
for he believes away
  what he nevertheless can see![9]

---

[9] Søren Kierkegaard, *Works of Love* (New York: HarperPerennial, 2009), 274.

Selected Readings for Further Study

† Ezekiel 18:30-32

† Mark 11:22-25

Questions for Reflection and Prayer:

1. Salvation requires repentance, for without it—as even the universalist, Aldous Huxley, was able to recognize—"there cannot be even a beginning of the spiritual life—for the life of the spirit is incompatible with the life of that 'old man,' whose acts, whose thoughts, whose very existence are the obstructing evils which have to be repented." Repentance then necessitates confession. And confession entails knowing our sin and acknowledging it before God. Do you "know" your sin? Have you, like David, openly acknowledged your sin before God?

2. Jesus reminds us that faith can move mountains. Has your faith brought you to the point where you have prayed for Christ to throw your mountain into the sea?

3. Kierkegaard says that forgiveness and sin exist in a relationship of faith. He says, "The unseen is in this that forgiveness takes away that which nevertheless is; the unseen is in this that what is seen nevertheless is not seen, for when it is seen, its not being seen is manifestly unseen....Just as one by faith *believes the unseen* in the seen, so the lover by forgiveness *believes* the seen away."

As Kierkegaard intimates, the real miracle in forgiveness is that God—who is both the Judge of our souls and the Lover of our hearts—forgives what He nevertheless can see. But though His love never fails, His forgiveness will not come into our lives until we confess our sin. Do you believe that God can forgive all that He sees in you? Have you become a "lover" like God—one who believes away what he nevertheless can see in himself? In others?

References
        Eze 18:30-32; Mk 11:22-25; 1 Cor 4:1-5

Diving Deeper:

1. J.D. Eubanks, MD, "Identity in Christ" in *More of Him, Less of Me* (Dawn Treader, LLC, 2018), 26.
2. Aldous Huxley, *The Perennial Philosophy* (New York: HarperPerennial, 2009), 256.
3. Søren Kierkegaard, *Works of Love* (New York: HarperPerennial, 2009), 273-4.

118

The Thirty-fifth Hour

Psalm 51:5-6—Surely I was sinful from birth,
  sinful from the time my mother conceived me.
  Surely you [Lord] desire truth in the inner parts;
  you teach me wisdom in the inmost place.

W hat is sin, O Lord,

that it should reach back into the womb,
with tendrils long enough
  to touch my first moment?
Is it possible that I trespassed against you
  before I even came
    screaming into this world,
red-faced, fist-bound, and kicking—
  full of protest from my first breath?
Was iniquity written into me
  like the blue of my eyes
    and the color of my skin,
so that when I do what I do not want to do,
  it only proves sin lives in me?
I tremble before you, O Lord,
  to think sin has been my longest companion,
    there since the time my mother conceived me.
For surely, if death came through sin,
  and all that lives slowly dies,
then sin is that monstrous hereditary
  passed down through the Fall—
    the corrupted nature no one escapes.

~

But why, O God, create something good,
  knowing full well,
    sin would make it anything but good?
Why give your conception over to Death,
  that in his grim work,
instead of life, he might conceive trouble
  and give birth to evil?
I cannot fathom why you would permit
  one man to bring death to many,

119

but that in the trespass of the one,
  a greater gift might come;
that in slavery to this law of sin,
  we might find eternal rescue
    from the body of death.
And why, Lord, if you are as good as you say,
  would you allow sin to increase,
unless its growing measure must be met
  with an overabundance of grace?
For where sin increased,
  grace increased all the more,
so that just as sin reigned in death,
    grace might reign in the righteousness
      that lifts us beyond the grave.

      ~

In this grace I now stand,
  a sinner who dies, but lives;
a slave still bound to the Fall,
  but ultimately free;
a heart whose beats diminish
  toward your determined end,
but a soul that goes on breathing
  in the eternity of now.

      ~

May your lamp, O Lord,
  search my spirit;
may your light shine
  on my inmost being.
For you, God, created my inner parts;
  you knit me together
    in my mother's womb.
And though sin seeks to unravel me,
  as it crowds and clouds your Truth,
may the glory of your Presence
  burn through to your first essence.
Be the blows and wounds that cleanse me;
    may your Word bring the gentle beatings
      that purge my inmost being,
till it takes on your perfection,
  full of the Spirit of life,
  who claims me incorruptible.

Selected Readings for Further Study

† Isaiah 59:1-8

† Romans 7:7-25

Questions for Reflection and Prayer:

1. The Doctrine of Original Sin is an unpleasant and sometimes contested biblical truth. But what evidences do we have that it is true? What does the Bible say? What do we see in the world around us that convinces us it must be true? And more importantly, what do we see within ourselves to bolster our conviction?

2. Is the Doctrine of Original Sin compatible with a loving God? Puritan preacher, Thomas Goodwin, says, "And that God ordained us thus to fall into sin and misery was but to illustrate the story of Christ's love, and thereby to render this our lover and husband the more glorious in his love to us, and to make this primitive condition whereunto God meant again to bring us the more eminently illustrious...." Does the presence of sin in the world allow us to know God's love in a richer and fuller way?

3. Biblically, death is linked to sin (Ro 5:12). As no one escapes death, then it follows that none are without sin (Ro 3:23). And as sin separates us from God, how shall we escape this "body of death"? Is death merely a natural phenomenon, or is it something more? For those who have been crucified with Christ (Gal 2:20)—who have died to themselves for Christ—what is the destiny of death in them? Christ defeated sin on the cross, and yet death remains in the world. Why? When and where will Death meets his final end (1 Cor 15:24-26)?

References
    Job 15:35; Isa 59:1-8; Ps 139:13; Pr 20:27, 30; Ro 5:1-21; 6:23; 7:7-25

Diving Deeper:

1. J.D. Eubanks, MD, "Right There With Me" in *More of Him, Less of Me* (Dawn Treader, LLC, 2018), 279.
2. Thomas Goodwin, *The Heart of Christ* (King Solomon, 2020), 60.

The Thirty-sixth Hour

Psalm 51:7-9—Cleanse me with hyssop, and I will be clean;
        wash me, and I will be whiter than snow.
    Let me hear joy and gladness;
        let the bones you [Lord] have crushed rejoice.
    Hide your face from my sins
        and blot out all my iniquity.

All have sinned

    and fall short of your glory, Lord.
For we are children who have chosen
    to roll our white clothes in the dirt;
we are offspring who have traded
    the mansion for the pigsty,
and the peace of the Father's house
    for the barnyard chaos.
Even creation reels from this fall;
    tethered to our choice,
        decay, death and pain plague nature too.
Only the snow seems to have held on
    to its heavenly clothes, O God.
Perhaps it alone has escaped the Fall,
    to fall instead as your gentle reminder
        of what purity once was, and still is—
the unblemished raiment of angels
    and the heavenly bodies to come—
white as your beard, gleaming as your robe,
    soft as your heart, blinding as the sun.

                    ~

When the land lies fallow and the trees barren—
    dark and brooding above,
        muddy and lifeless below—
you open your heavenly storehouses, O Lord,
    to shower your frozen water
        down upon the dying.
And in the morning, all things are new,
    washed in the wonder of white,
        covered in the blanket of Heaven.
I long to be clothed in the color of snow,
    dressed in the brilliance of your promise.

122

For though my sins are like scarlet,
   you say, they shall be white as snow;
though my transgressions are red as crimson,
   you promise, they shall be like wool.
Will you cleanse me with hyssop, O Lord?
   Will you wash my bloody body
      in the ashen water of forgiveness?
For if you do not stoop down to bathe me,
   how will I ever be clean?
And if you do not wash me,
   how will I ever be part of you?
For you, O Lord, cannot dwell with sin,
   and your holiness demands holiness.
Your eyes are too pure to look on evil,
   and you cannot tolerate wrong.
Where then is my hope, O God?
   Is it not with the One
      who is coming on the clouds?
When I see Him, shall I not be like Him?
   Will I not be purified as He is pure?
For to the pure, all things are pure;
   blessed are the pure, for they will see God.

                    ~

Cleanse me and purify me, O Lord, I pray;
   sanctify me by your Truth;
      justify me by your Name.
May your blood wash my scarlet white;
   may your angel of death pass me by;
      may the Destroyer see the blood on my door.
Then I will sing of your deliverance;
   and the one you have crushed
      will have cause to rejoice.
For though weeping and bitterness
   surround me,
      your love, O Lord, will sustain me.
Though the kingdom of this world
   wails a wail it refuses to hear,
through the deafening noise I catch
   your well-spring of joy and gladness.
I hear the whisper of your eternal song,
   and it is sweeter than honey to my soul.

<u>Selected Readings for Further Study</u>

† Numbers 19:1-10

† Luke 15:11-32

<u>Questions for Reflection and Prayer:</u>

1. In viewing Rembrandt's *Prodigal Son*, priest and author, Henri Nouwen, is caused to consider whom he is more like: the younger or the elder son. A friend then says to him, "Whether you are the younger son or the elder son, you have to realize that you are called to become the father."
   In the Parable of the Lost Son, which of the characters can you identify with? Have you been prodigal with the Father's gifts? Maybe you've been angry and ungenerous in your evaluation of God's grace in the life of another? Perhaps you, like the Father, have had the opportunity to forgive a great wrong done to you?

2. In the Old Testament, the water of cleansing was used for the purification of sin (Nu 19:1-10). Is there any further need for this ritual washing? And if not, why? Do we need to be washed at all?

3. During the Passover, the blood painted on the doorframe with a hyssop branch was the salvation of the Jews (Ex 12:22-23). Has your "doorframe" been painted in the blood of the Lamb? Have you felt the Destroyer pass your door?

References
   Ex 12:22-23; Nu 19:1-10; Isa 1:16-18; Jer 4:14; Hab 1:13; Lk 15:11-25; Jn 13:8; Acts 22:16; Ro 3:23; 1 Cor 6:11; Titus 1:15; Heb 9:19; 1 Jn 3:3;

<u>Diving Deeper:</u>

1. J.D. Eubanks, MD, "God of Peace" in *More of Him, Less of Me* (Dawn Treader, LLC, 2018), 127.
2. Henri Nouwen, *The Return of the Prodigal Son* (New York: Image Books, 1994), 22.

124

The Thirty-seventh Hour

Psalm 51:10—Create in me a pure heart, O God,
and renew a steadfast spirit within me.

Nicodemus, Nicodemus,

how my heart goes out to you!
For what private pain pulled you
into a midnight rendezvous
with the Revealer of mysteries!
I have been with you in the darkness,
confused, amazed, and aghast—
puzzled to the point of perplexity.
For the Rabbi takes purity
from our soiled, but busy hands,
and wants, it seems, to throw it
back into the womb,
demanding we be born again.
But by what magic can a man climb
back into the watery world
from which he emerged?
Shall the clocks turn around,
and all that lives in me
live itself in reverse,
running backwards to my genesis
in desperate hope of a fresh start?
When the water bursts again,
will I enter this world with eyes
to see the unseen Kingdom?
And who is to say,
that it won't all run amok again?
For will God bind the serpent now,
or will he go on slithering toward the fire?
Shall the straightened be straight forever,
or will the crooked work its way in?
Perhaps straight is only straight,
when the crooked is crooked;
and who but the Lord can straighten
what His hands have bent?

~

Whether of flesh or spirit,
  we are born of water.
But flesh gives birth to flesh,
  and Spirit gives birth to spirit.
Lord, in this hour, hear my prayer—
  take my heart of stone
  and give me a heart of flesh.
Create in me a new spirit, O God,
  undivided in its devotion,
    steadfast in its trajectory—
    the crooked made arrow straight.
May the pulse of my life
  be as unerring as your rhythm.
For you, Lord, became a thumping heart,
  born of the Spirit;
your love never skipped a beat,
  until your heart burst forth
    with blood and water.
Through these fluids we must emerge—
  not from the womb,
    but from our dark depths—
to breathe true life's first breath,
  in a world drenched in your light.
Born of Spirit, we are spirit;
  and while we still swim in turbulent seas,
    the depths cannot claim us.
For we are now buoyed by your breath—
  the old has gone, the new has come.
            ~
Nicodemus, Nicodemus,
  how my heart goes out to you!
For you sought Him in your depths;
  you swam with a curious might,
    up toward that glorious Light.
But did you dare your first breath?
  Did you emerge from the water,
    gasping into the Kingdom of Light?
Were you born again in that breath of belief
  that declared its love in strips of linen
    and a mixture of myrrh and aloes?
When all things are new, Nicodemus,
  and mystery melts in revelation,
    may I see Christ in you!

126

Selected Readings for Further Study

† Ezekiel 11:16-21

† John 3:1-21

Questions for Reflection and Prayer:

1. As the Apostle John tells the story, Nicodemus has a hard time understanding Christ's command to be "born again." What does it mean to be "born again"? How does it happen? What happens if it doesn't happen? According to Jesus, how do we obtain eternal life? What is the "ticket to Heaven"?

2. Jesus was conceived of the Holy Spirit, and yet He was a man. You are a man or woman, but have you been born of the Spirit? What does Jesus mean when He says the "Spirit gives birth to spirit"?

3. When God promises through Ezekiel to give the people of Israel an "undivided heart," what does He mean? With the undivided heart comes a new spirit. Does that Spirit live in you? Is your heart undivided in its devotion to God? Anglican priest, William Law, describes this devotion:

> He therefore is the devout man, who lives no longer to his own will, or the way and spirit of the world, but to the sole will of God, who considers God in everything, who serves God in everything, who makes all the parts of his common life, parts of piety, by doing everything in the nature of God, and under such rules as are comformable to His glory.

Are you living to the "sole will of God"?

References
    Ecc 7:13; Eze 11:19-20; Jn 3:1-21; 19:38-42; 2 Cor 5:17; Gal 6:15; Eph 4:22-24; Col 3:9-10

Diving Deeper:

1. J.D. Eubanks, MD, "Binding Love" in *More of Him, Less of Me* (Dawn Treader, LLC, 2018), 56.
2. J.D. Eubanks, MD, "Undivided Devotion" in *Twelve Stones: Apologetics for an Age of Relativism* (Dawn Treader, LLC, 2022), 127-147.
3. William Law, *A Serious Call to a Devout and Holy Life* (Mineola, NY: Dover Publications, 2013), 1.

Psalm 51:11—Do not cast me from your [the Lord's] Presence
or take your Holy Spirit from me.

W hat greater punishment, O God,

could you mete out upon me,
  than to cast me from your Presence?
For wasn't this the lot of the Liar,
  that angel of light
    who aspired to your throne—
that prince of darkness who dared
  to war against Heaven's matchless King—
until cast from gleaming courts,
  Satan fell from the clouds,
    like a lightening bolt from the Storm?
Surely your Word promises your enemies
  nothing less than the slippery ground
    of a pride and ambition that casts down.
What befell the Liar, might befall the man;
  and the one who bargains with the devil,
    will one day join him in liquid fire.
For the false prophets and wayward priests
    are angelic blackguards dressed in flesh,
  who weave the deceiver's yarn—
one day, they will be cast out and forgotten,
  into a darkness filled with nothing
    but everlasting shame.

~

But though I have sinned against you, O Lord,
  I am not an enemy to your throne.
For I would rather serve my King on earth,
  than reign in the halls of hell.
So what will of mine still remains,
  I set like flint to conquer in your Name.
For you sit high and exalted in my heart,
  and the train of your robe fills my temple.
Your Spirit gives me life,
  and the breath I breathe, I breathe in you.
If you take your Spirit from me, God,
  you threaten to take my life;

128

and if you quit my temple's court,
  my body will be an empty universe,
filled with prayers that go on racing
  into an endless darkness.
      ~
O Lord, I know you know my sin,
  for your Spirit searches all things:
from the canyon channels of my heart,
  to the deep things of God—
    nothing is hidden from your sight.
A man's spirit may know his thoughts,
  and however vile the wanderings,
    his spirit might trace every turn.
But no one knows your thoughts, O God,
  save the Spirit you deposit
    as a guarantee of what is to come—
      sealed by you, for you.
So if you withdraw, how will I understand;
  if you depart, will wisdom turn to foolishness?
And if you steal your Spirit away, Lord,
  will I not fall into that black hole of the soul
    from which even light cannot escape?
No, Lord, do not threaten to leave me;
  do not lift your seal from my heart.
Stay forever in the temple you have made;
  sit on the throne you have fashioned.
Forgive me for the sin that saddens you,
  for the insolence that seeks your throne.
And even if you must cast me out, O Lord,
  let it be as that prodigal nation
    you soon bring back in love.
Remember your words of lamentation
  and the promises you spoke through tears—
For men are not cast off
  by the Lord forever.
Though He brings grief, He will show compassion,
  so great is His unfailing love.
For he does not willingly bring affliction
  or grief to the children of men.
In my grief, show me your compassion, O Lord;
  in my affliction, unveil your love.

<u>Selected Readings for Further Study</u>

† Isaiah 14:12-15

† 1 Corinthians 2:10-16

<u>Questions for Reflection and Prayer:</u>

1. In *Paradise Lost*, John Milton's Satan says, "To reign is worth ambition, though in hell./ Better to reign in hell than serve in heaven." Satan was cast down from Heaven for this impudence. Have you, like the devil, determined that your will will be "unconquerable"? Or have you chosen to align your will with Heaven's, to serve the "matchless King"? Will you serve Christ on earth, or do you seek, like the devil, to reign in hell?

2. Have you considered what your life would be like without God's Spirit in you? If the mere thought of His absence does not horrify you, then it might be worth asking: Is the Spirit in my life at all?

3. The Spirit gives us life and is God's deposit in us, guaranteeing what is to come. The Spirit is also His seal of ownership in our lives (2 Cor 1:22). Does your life bear the seal of Heaven? And if so, what does that mean for today? For tomorrow?

References
> Job 33:4; Ps 71:9; 73:18-20; Isa 14:12-15; Jer 23:33-40; La 3:31-33; Lk 10:18; Jn 6:63; 1 Cor 2:10-16; 6:19; 2 Cor 1:22; Eph 1:14

<u>Diving Deeper:</u>

1. J.D. Eubanks, MD, "Personal Ascendency" in *More of Him, Less of Me* (Dawn Treader, LLC, 2018), 381.
2. John Milton, *Paradise Lost* (London: Arcturus, 2014), 20.

Psalm 51:12—Restore to me the joy of your [the Lord's] salvation
and grant me a willing spirit to sustain me.

O Lord, you have worn me out;

I have been battered to a pulp;
I am weary beyond words.
No doubt, my sin is to blame,
  and the faintness I feel
    is but my sickness within.
I do not know why these trials come,
  but one thing I do—
    I have nothing left.
Yet what little speech remains,
  offers up to you this plea.
In the desperate hope of David,
  I ask you to relent—"*Who knows?*
    The Lord may be gracious to me...."
For I am that stumbling runner
  who has run his race so hard,
  he staggers in view of the finish—
    Have I run in vain?
I am that beleaguered pugilist,
  now crouched in the corner,
    bludgeoned to bleeding,
  teetering on tottering—
    Have I fought a good fight?
I am that exhausted prophet
  who merely wished to die—
"*I have had enough, Lord. Take my life!*"
For like your weary seer, O God,
  I'm too tired to care, much less to will.
I know your promises, I recite your words;
  yet in my fatigue I cannot rise
    from the shade of your broom tree.
But for reasons I can't fathom,
  some force from my depths still prays
    for a willing spirit to sustain me. Why?

131

For when I consider the relentless struggle,
  it seems absurd to keep on going.
I know exhaustion is my enemy's weapon,
  and the endless siege he lays
    is his greatest hope for my ruin.
But why should I desire to rise again,
  if the blows will only keep coming?
Why live simply to live a life
  hell-bent on shipwrecking hope?
For what does tomorrow promise,
  but the burden of more brokenness?
Should I care when no one else does;
  should I stand against a relentless tide?
When the others have walked away,
  when they say in their hearts, "I will not,"
  must I be the one left who says, "I will"?
And for that matter, what is the will of man,
  that life should depend so heavily upon it?
Why, God, allow anything to stand
  gatekeeper to your sustaining grace?
No, my Lord, knock my gates down;
  commandeer my unwilling will!
May your sustaining grace burst through
  what ravaged will of mine remains.
Throw back the stone once again
  and stride forth from the tomb.
Restore in me the awe and wonder
  of my first encounter;
fill me with the trembling delight
  that sends me running with exclamation!
Draw joy from the well of your salvation
  and pour it down my parched throat.
For your friend is too feeble to lift his head
  and gulp your goodness down.
Lay yourself upon my listless soul,
  mouth to mouth, eyes to eyes, hands to hands—
  resurrect this sleeping child.
Then will I rise rejoicing in the Lord;
  I will be joyful in God my Savior.
For the Sovereign Lord is my sustainer,
    the One who whispers in love,
    "I have made you and I will carry you;
    I will sustain you and I will rescue you."

132

Selected Readings for Further Study

† 1 Kings 19:1-9

† Matthew 28:1-10

Questions for Reflection and Prayer:

1. Have you had a moment in your life like Elijah's under the shade of a desert broom tree? Have you run your race to the point of staggering? Did God meet you in your weakness? Can Elijah's weakness be a source of encouragement to you?

2. Christ promised His disciples a life full of troubles (Jn 16:33). Those ceaseless troubles can fatigue us. And fatigue is one of the greatest weapons of the devil. What must be our defense?

3. G.K. Chesterton says, "Joy…is the gigantic secret of the Christian." But we are wrong to think this joy will *always* be an ebullience of spirit. Sometimes Christian joy—especially in our seasons of exhaustion—might hope to look more like Ignatius' "consolation" of spirit:

> ….he [the Lord] gives…interior consolation, which casts out all disturbance and draws us into total love of the Lord….With this divine consolation, all hardships are ultimately pleasure, all fatigues rest. For anyone who proceeds with this interior fervour, warmth and consolation, there is no load so great that it does not seem light to them, nor any penance or other hardship so great that it is not very sweet.

Have you asked the Lord to bring you His "interior consolation"?

References
    2 Sam 12:1-23; 1 Ki 19:1-9; 2 Ki 4:34; Isa 12:3, 46:4; Hab 3:17; Mt 28:1-10

Diving Deeper:

1. J.D. Eubanks, MD, "Comfort in Weakness" in *More of Him, Less of Me* (Dawn Treader, LLC, 2018), 342.
2. J.D. Eubanks, MD, "Mouth to Mouth, Eyes to Eyes, Hands to Hands" in *More of Him, Less of Me* (Dawn Treader, LLC, 2018), 282.
3. G.K. Chesterton, *Orthodoxy* (Peabody: Hendrickson Publishers, 2006), 155.
4. Saint Ignatius of Loyola, *Personal Writings* (New York: Penguin Books, 1996), 132-133.

The Fortieth Hour

Psalm 51:13-15—Then I will teach transgressors your [the Lord's] ways,
and sinners will turn back to you.
Save me from bloodguilt, O God,
the God who saves me,
and my tongue will sing of your righteousness.
O Lord, open my lips,
and my mouth will declare your praise.

In cold blood I stand

a murderous man,
soaked in bloodguilt.
For where the knife has failed
to plunge into flesh,
the mind has dared the deed,
the heart committed the crime.
Many times have I said, *"You fool!"*
and many more
have I claimed her with my eyes.
I have longed with jealous sorrow
for things I do not have,
twisted truths to fit my interests,
and spurned your gracious rest, O God.
Lord, apart from your grace,
my righteous acts are but filthy rags—
my soul shrivels up like a leaf let go.
For even my best efforts are woven
with the fatal thread of me;
and the road to hell is paved,
not only in jealously, blood, and lies,
but also good intentions.
~
If the mind is what matters,
and the heart is what counts,
where is the man who can stand
innocent before you, O God?
For no man can tame the tongue,
much less the fickle wanderings
of his unruly thoughts.

134

And unless we throw God down
  in the tyranny of deluded fictions,
there is no escape from sin,
  and no shelter from the coming storm.
For even if my waking hours
  were perfectly mastered,
who will keep my dreams
  from trespassing against you, God?
I may be one man by day,
  and quite another at night.
Must I then gouge out my eye
  and cut off my right hand?
If I walk through the world
  maimed for righteousness,
    would the midnight fail to betray me?

~

O God, will you take me just as I am,
  a man of impure thoughts
    and imperfect deeds?
Wouldn't it be better to resonant your voice
  in this soiled vessel,
    so all might know the Glory is you?
For surely men loathe perfection,
  and a convincing witness
    cannot be too clean.
Your best servant is the suffering one;
    the disciple whose song rings most true,
      is never far from the muddy mire
  you pulled him from.
Rescue me then, O King of Heaven;
  reach down and pull me up.
May my life be the tarnished horn
  you use to trumpet your praise.
Redeem my every truant thought,
  transform my wayward heart.
May my imperfect soul be the soil
  for the seeds of your coming Kingdom.
Sprout in me an invincible work
  that causes even the vilest to say,
  "Great is the Lord,
    and greatly is He to be praised!"

Selected Readings for Further Study

† Exodus 20:1-17

† Matthew 5:17-30

Questions for Reflection and Prayer:

1. It goes without saying: The Ten Commandments are impossible to keep. Should we despair? Our nation tears these commandments down from public places. Are they irrelevant? Concerning this Law, the Apostle Paul says to the Galatian Church: "...the law was put in charge to lead us to Christ that we might be justified by faith" (Gal 3:24). Have you allowed the Law to lead you to Christ today?

2. Jesus makes sin against God much more than what we actually *do* in the visible world. Why does the unseen territory of the mind and heart matter so much?

3. Knowing God cares about the sin of our thought lives can be terrifying. It might bring us to despair. But Andrew Murray helps us frame these fears when he draws a distinction between *voluntary* and *involuntary* sins. Murray says, "even in one who is walking in true obedience, evil suggestions of pride, unloving, or impure thoughts, over which the mind has no direct control" will inevitability emerge in our minds, waking or sleeping. We have no conscious control of these random thoughts. As a result, they are not "imputed as acts of transgressions." Christ's blood covers these.

But *voluntary* sins—sins of willful transgression—are another matter. God does hold us accountable for these sins. And though the blood of Christ may cover these sins as well, we must repent of them and war against them in our lives.

Have you made a habit of warring against the *voluntary* sin in your life?

References
        Ex 20:1-17; Ps 145:3; Isa 64:6; Mt 5:17-30; Gal 3:24

Diving Deeper:

1. J.D. Eubanks, MD, "The One Who Came Back" in *More of Him, Less of Me* (Dawn Treader, LLC, 2018), 207.
2. J.D. Eubanks, MD, *Gentlest of Ways* (Dawn Treader, LLC, 2020), 102.
3. Andrew Murray, *A Life of Obedience* (Minneapolis, MN: Bethany House, 2004), 62-63.

The Forty-first Hour

Psalm 51:16-17—You [Lord] do not delight in sacrifice, or I would bring it;
you do not take pleasure in burnt offerings.
The sacrifices of God are a broken spirit,
a broken and contrite heart,
O God, you will not despise.

High and lofty One,

He who lives forever, whose Name is holy:
the Lord who lives in a high and exalted place—
Heaven of heaven's heaven—
above the mounting clouds,
beyond the distant stars,
third in the trinity of the sky—
few, O God—whether in the body or spirit—
have glimpsed you in your paradise.
Will the Lord of this inexpressible place
choose to dwell in a broken man?
For if the highest heaven cannot contain you,
will there be room enough
in the drab inn of my heart?
And why would your Majesty
choose to rest in this lowly place?
For tired and weathered as it is,
my heart is anything but your throne room—
gilded in jasper, carnelian, and emerald,
announced by thunder, lit up by lightening,
fanned by the wings of creatures singing,
'Holy, holy, holy,
is the Lord God Almighty,
who was, and is, and is to come."
~

O Lord, the Everlasting King—
the Almighty God who created us
for His renown and praise and honor—
will you be angry with me forever,
and allow my enemies to go unchallenged?
Surely you can see my spirit grows faint
and my breathing shallow.

137

Perhaps you do not relent
  because I haven't suffered enough pain
    to know your joy.
For are not pain and joy
    cut of the same cloth?
  Do they not often proceed hand in hand?
Maybe the chasm of my remorse
  is not yet deep enough to be filled by you,
  and my contrition still too full of me.
Maybe I have not yet come
  to the divine meridian
where my spiritual shadow vanishes,
  and I become almost nothing—
nothing but an empty room
    to be filled by you.[10]

              ~

The one you esteem, O Lord,
  trembles at your word.
The place where you choose to dwell
  is the humble and contrite heart.
Heaven is your throne,
  the earth is your footstool.
With this ground beneath your feet,
  feel my quaking body with your toes.
In your great mercy,
  peer through the smoke
  of my meaningless sacrifices.
And though the room of my heart
  may not yet fit your royal standards,
  please condescend to its humble walls.
For if you do not come quickly,
  to revive the spirit of the lowly
  and rejuvenate the heart of the contrite,
this shoddy place may fall apart
  for want of your healing touch.
Though you have seen my ways,
  O Lord, stoop down to heal me;
guide me to the comfort and peace
  that puts praise on mourning lips.

---

[10] C.S. Lewis, *The Collected Letters of C.S. Lewis, Vol III* in *The Business of Heaven* (New York: HarperCollins, 1984), 221-222.

138

Selected Readings for Further Study

† Isaiah 57:14-21

† Revelation 4:1-11

Questions for Reflection and Prayer:

1. In recent times, there has been much talk about NDE's (near death experiences). Regardless of what one thinks about the veracity of such experiences, the Apostle Paul gives us a similar story in 2 Corinthians 12:1-5. What things do we learn about Heaven in this account?

2. Mother Teresa says, "Prayer enlarges the heart until it is capable of containing God's gift of Himself. Ask and seek, and your heart will grow big enough to receive Him and keep Him as your own." Do you believe the room of your heart is capable of expanding to God-size proportions?

3. The Old Testament prophets repeatedly remind us: God does not need our sacrifices, but desires our hearts, broken and contrite before Him. What is contrition? Are you bringing your broken and contrite spirit before the Lord today?

References
        Isa 57:14-21; 66:2; Jer 13:11; 2 Cor 12:1-5; Rev 4:1-11

Diving Deeper:

1. J.D. Eubanks, MD, "Room in the Inn of the Heart" in *More of Him, Less of Me* (Dawn Treader, LLC, 2018), 210.
2. C.S. Lewis, *The Collected Letters of C.S. Lewis, Vol III* in *The Business of Heaven* (New York: HarperCollins, 1984), 221-222.
3. Malcolm Muggeridge, *Something Beautiful for God* (New York: HarperCollins, 1971), 66.

Psalm 51:18-19—In your [the Lord's] good pleasure make Zion prosper;
build up the walls of Jerusalem.
Then there will be righteous sacrifices,
whole burnt offerings to delight you;
then bulls will be offered on your altar.

Zion, you are the jewel

in the Lord's signet ring;
City of God, City of Truth,
Holy Mountain drenched in blood,
but crowned in promise.
You have killed your prophets
and stoned your messengers.
Even your King you hung upon a tree—
mocked with a crown of thorns,
pierced with your hypocrisy.
But the blood your blindness shed, Zion,
has become the tested Stone;
your ignorance has proved God's wisdom,
and your insolence, His limitless grace.
For if you had only known
what would bring you peace,
wouldn't your walls have cried out,
"Blessed is the King who comes
in the name of the Lord!
Peace in Heaven
and glory in the highest!"
Even so, Jerusalem, O Jerusalem,
amidst the rubble of your ruin,
a precious Cornerstone has been laid—
a sure foundation established.
~
Shall we remain a heap of charred stone,
or will we choose to build again?
In the good pleasure of God,
let us raise walls upon the Rock!
For until our hearts cry out again,
"Blessed is He who comes in the name of the Lord!"
the war will never stop, the enemy never tire.

140

But on that glorious day, O Jerusalem,
when the sky falls and the sea vanishes—
and only peace remains—
you will be a bride coming down,
beautifully dressed for your Husband.
You shall descend from Heaven,
adorned in perfection
and clothed in the glory of God.
For all things will be made new,
so that even you, Daughter of Zion,
will have every tear wiped from your eyes—
save those that drip from joy.
~

Yet until God dwells with men again,
what sacrifices shall we bring,
what songs shall we sing?
Does the Lord of Zion
delight in burnt offerings and sacrifices
as much as obeying His voice?
"*If you love me*," says the Lord,
"*you will obey what I command*";
and "*to obey is better than sacrifice,
and to heed is better than the fat of rams.*"
For loveless duty may flow
in the blood of slaughtered bulls,
but the beating of God's heart
pulses with the living sacrifice
of a life lived out in love.
For not even the blood of my firstborn
could cover my transgressions;
the fruit of my body
could never atone for my soul.
God alone stays the knife,
and He has provided the Lamb—
bleating in the thicket,
bleeding on the cross.
Salvation has come to you, O Zion,
gentle and riding on a donkey;
and in God's great love,
He has shown us what is good,
He has told me what I must do—
*to act justly and to love mercy
and to walk humbly with my God.*

Selected Readings for Further Study

† 1 Samuel 15:1-31

† Revelation 21:1-5

Questions for Reflection and Prayer:

1. The city of Jerusalem is a historically and spiritually singular place. Despite its turbulent past—and its religiously and politically contentious present—it is God's chosen city. Sometimes the Bible uses "Zion" to represent God's people as well. How is your spiritual life like the city of Zion? Can God's promise for Jerusalem be a source of hope for you today?

2. King Saul failed, not because of a failure of religious duty, but rather a lack of obedience (1 Sam 15). What does his story teach us about God's heart for obedience? How do Jesus' words in John 14 further inform us?

3. God still requires sacrifice from His people. But although that sacrifice no longer requires the blood of animals, it is now arguably more personal and more costly. God invites us to present our bodies to Him as "living sacrifices." We must let go before the Kingdom can manifest in us. Aldous Huxley summarizes it well:

> "Our kingdom go" is the necessary and unavoidable corollary of "Thy kingdom come." For the more there is of self, the less there is of God. The divine eternal fullness of life can be gained only by those who have deliberately lost the partial, separative life of craving and self-interest, of egocentric thinking, feeling, wishing and acting.

Have you made of habit of "Our kingdom go"?

References
    1 Sam 15: 22-23; Ps 2:6; 14:7; 50:2; ; 76:2; 87:3; 110:2; Isa 28:16; 59:20;
    La 2; Joel 3:16; Mic 6:6-8; Zec 8:1-3; 9:9; Mt 23:37-39; Lk 19:38-44;
    Ro 12:1-8; Rev 21:1-4

Diving Deeper:

1. J.D. Eubanks, MD, "Living Sacrifices" in *More of Him, Less of Me* (Dawn Treader, LLC, 2018), 251.
2. J.D. Eubanks, MD, *For the Joy of Obeying* (Dawn Treader, LLC, 2019), 68-76.
3. Aldous Huxley, *The Perennial Philosophy* (New York: HarperPerennial, 2009), 96.

V.

Psalm 102

A prayer of an afflicted man. When he is faint
and pours out his lament before the Lord.

Hear my prayer, O Lord;
  let my cry for help come to you.
Do not hide your face from me
  when I am in distress.
Turn your ear to me;
  when I call, answer me quickly.
For my days vanish like smoke;
  my bones burn like glowing embers.
My heart is blighted and withered like grass;
  I forget to eat my food.
Because of my loud groaning
  I am reduced to skin and bones.
I am like a desert owl,
  like a bird alone on a roof.
All day long my enemies taunt me;
  those who rail against me use my name as a curse.
For I eat ashes as my food
  and mingle my drink with tears
because of your great wrath,
  for you have taken me up and thrown me aside.
My days are like the evening shadow;
  I wither away like grass.
But you, O Lord, sit enthroned forever;
  your renown endures through all generations.
You will arise and have compassion on Zion,
  for it is time to show favor to her;
  the appointed time has come.
For her stones are dear to your servants;
  her very dust moves them to pity.

The nations will fear the Name of the Lord,
   all the kings of the earth will revere your glory.
For the Lord will rebuild Zion
   and appear in His glory.
He will respond to the prayer of the destitute;
   He will not despise their plea.
Let this be written for a future generation,
   that a people not yet created may praise the Lord:
"The Lord looked down from His sanctuary on high,
   from Heaven He viewed the earth,
to hear the groans of the prisoners
   and release those condemned to death."
So the Name of the Lord will be declared in Zion
   and His praise in Jerusalem
when the peoples and the kingdoms
   assemble to worship the Lord.
In the course of my life He broke my strength;
   He cut short my days.
So I said:
   "Do not take me away, O my God, in the
      midst of my days;
   your years go on through all generations.
In the beginning you laid the foundations of the earth,
   and the heavens are the work of your hands.
They will perish, but you remain;
   they will all wear out like a garment.
Like clothing you will change them
   and they will be discarded.
But you remain the same,
   and your years will never end.
The children of your servants will live in your Presence;
   their descendants will be established before you."

The Forty-third Hour

Psalm 102:1-3—Hear my prayer, O Lord;
    let my cry for help come to you.
    Do not hide your face from me
    when I am in distress.
    Turn your ear to me;
    when I call, answer me quickly.

O Lord, I cry out to you,

my spirit pours forth in prayer;
reckless and perhaps feckless
   words tumble off my tongue—
     candid complaints pester your door.
But will you unlock the latch to let me in?
   Will you give me your ear
    to bend at my will?
Or must I be satisfied
   to speak into the silent void,
trusting you are listening to my lament
   through all those layers between us?
In this hour, I confess, O Lord,
   to a certain lack of certainty,
and the ancients' sureness of hope
   seems like a marvelous myth.
Will you let me glimpse your face
   to convince me you are not hiding?
Can you speak into my darkness
   to persuade me I still hear?
For of what substance
   do you think I'm made, Lord,
   to require of me a boundless faith,
when even Moses and Elijah stood before your fire,
   and your blinding power conversed with Saul?
And though Abraham waited decades
   to see you answer his prayers,
your promises were proceeded by your Presence,

145

as you passed before him
   in a smoking firepot with blazing torch.
Compared to these living pillars of faith,
   I am a scrawny child, blindfolded and twisted around,
      whom you've then asked to do a terrifying thing—
to see in everything the hand of Everything,
   and to draw from a disembodied silence
      declarations of an unending love.
But even the stray dog might howl his protest
   before the man in the moon,
and his pitiful complaint seldom fails
   to fall on listening ears that move.
Yet though I moan into the moonlight,
   I have yet to see you darken my door;
though I cry out in my weariness,
   my prayers feel like dead letters.
This is the great gamble—
   to believe in the One I cannot see.
Even so, I suppose there is nothing to lose
   in unburdening my soul before you.
For if you exist at all, Lord,
   then you must know my thoughts
   before a word is on my lips,
and no mumbled jumble of diction
   will fail to send its message through.
And if by chance you aren't behind the door,
   and what I thought was a dialogue with Love
   only opens to an empty darkness,
then at least I've been a self-soothing child
   finding some comfort in soft soliloquies.
So I will pray the prayer of the penitent;
   I will bemoan to the God
      who dared to become a man.
Because if that mystery is true, *everything changes*—
   and even though He is now in Heaven,
      His heart *is* here with me—
      for His perfection destroys not His affections.[11]

---

[11] Thomas Goodwin, *The Heart of Christ* (Oviedo-Asturias (Spain): King Solomon, 2020), 95.

Selected Readings for Further Study

† Genesis 15:1-21

† Acts 9:1-9

Questions for Reflection and Prayer:

1. When Jesus raises Lazarus from the tomb, He says, "Father, I thank you that you have heard me. I knew that you always hear me, but I said this for the benefit of the people standing here…."(Jn 11:42). Christ had confidence that the Father heard His prayers. Do you?

2. In comparing our contemporary culture's "think" to previous ones, Thomas Howard says, "The myth sovereign in the old age was that everything means everything. The myth sovereign in the new is that nothing means anything." Which culture have you chosen to plant your flag in?

3. Philosopher Paul Tillich recognizes the incredible challenge of faith. He says, "The risk to faith in one's ultimate concern is indeed the greatest risk man can run. For if it proves to be a failure, the meaning of one's life breaks down…." Have you taken the great gamble of faith, or are you still holding on to your cards? For the one who refuses to bet on Christ, what are the potential costs?

References
Ge 15:1-21; Ex 3:1-17; 1 Ki 18:38; Ps 139:4; Jn 11:42; Acts 9:1-19

Diving Deeper:

1. J.D. Eubanks, MD, "Living Letters" in *More of Him, Less of Me* (Dawn Treader, LLC, 2018), 221.
2. Thomas Howard, *Chance or the Dance* (San Francisco: Ignatius Press, 2018), 2.
3. Paul Tillich, *Dynamics of Faith* (New York: HarperCollins, 2009), 21.

The Forty-fourth Hour

Psalm 102:3-5—For my days vanish like smoke;
my bones burn like glowing embers.
My heart is blighted and withered like grass;
I forget to eat my food.
Because of my loud groaning
I am reduced to skin and bones.

Healer of the heart, O God,

you are the lover of my leprous soul.
You are the Great Physician,
who sees in blight only possibility;
in endless bleeding, the reach of mercy;
and in the odor of death,
nothing but the sweet tears of resurrection.
You came with your immortal medicine,
not for those who think themselves healthy,
but for the ones who know they are sick.
Sin is the sickness that afflicts us—
the pestilence of our darkness.
Canker of the heart, plague of the spirit,
we can run, but we cannot hide—
till we hide ourselves in you, Lord.

~

It is a simple thing really—
to be cleansed—
to dip down into the Jordan;
to walk into the water
covered in the untouchable sickness,
only to emerge spotlessly clean
with the skin of a young boy.
Simple and yet so hard—
for though I have your prescription, Lord,
you will not force me to follow it.
And I would rather you met me on my ground,
to wave your hands over me—

148

touch me if you must—
and then send me on my merry way.
Yet you demand so much more—
the consciousness of my bottomless iniquity,
and the utter futility of every other effort.
These milestones must be met,
before I will walk into your cleansing current.
But perhaps the greater courage comes
in stepping back onto the shore—
for then the journey of belief begins.
For it is one thing to be healed of a disease,
and quite another to believe
this healing heals it all.
How can one treatment cover every sickness,
unless every sickness is really one in the same?
How can one remedy work on every man,
unless the Man with the remedy
takes on everyman's sickness?

~

From a distance your forgiveness, O Lord,
is a fairytale full of lovable magic.
But up close and personal,
it is a hard pill to swallow down
for the man who is nothing
but skin, bones and groans.
For how few blighted hearts
have the strength and courage to believe,
your forgiveness means forgotten?
And yet it is true:
when you forgive, you forget;
when you heal, it is healed—
you turn your back on our black.
But great consolation means great demand—
for my forgiveness depends upon my forgiveness,
and the gift you so freely give
is one of the hardest to give in return.
O Lord, your mercy presents no greater challenge—
the litmus of my likeness to Christ:
To forgive as I have been forgiven by you.

149

Selected Readings for Further Study

† 2 Kings 5

† Hebrews 10:1-18

<u>Questions for Reflection and Prayer:</u>

1. Naaman, the leprous commander from Aram, almost fails to be healed from his leprosy because of an unwillingness to do the simple thing asked of him: wash in the Jordan River. Are you blocking God's healing in your life because you too are resisting doing the simple thing He asks of you?

2. Kierkegaard says, "For *at a distance* men see Christianity as a lovable thing," but "...*at close range* Christianity is hateful and shocking." What do you think Kierkegaard is trying to articulate? In what ways is the Christian faith *both* lovable and simultaneously hateful and shocking?

3. C.S. Lewis says, "If you don't forgive you will not be forgiven. No part of His [Christ's] teaching is dearer, and there are no exceptions to it." Have you considered that your forgiveness is contingent upon your forgiveness of others? How might this change the way you live today?

Reflections
　　　2 Ki 5; Mk 5:21-34; Jn 11:1-44; Lk 5:31; Heb 10:1-18

<u>Diving Deeper:</u>

1. J.D. Eubanks, MD, "The Simple Things" in *More of Him, Less of Me* (Dawn Treader, LLC, 2018), 17.
2. Søren Kierkegaard, *The Diary of Søren Kierkegaard* (New York: Citadel Press, 1988), 150.
3. C.S. Lewis, *The Weight of Glory* (New York: HarperCollins, 2001), 178.

The Forty-fifth Hour

Psalm 102:6-7—I am like a desert owl,
like an owl among the ruins.
I lie awake; I have become
like a bird alone on a roof.

You are a jealous lover, O Lord,

a God of unbridled passion—
a lover whose love is only love,
when it makes us or takes us.
For love is nothing
but a half-hearted imposter,
if it does not have the strength
to destroy us.
If it is a love that only sweetly sings
and adorns us with its many jewels,
but does not wield hands
powerful enough to ravage us
in its desolating anger,
then it will never hope to posses
the fortitude to stay on
in stormy days and silent nights.
In the solitude of your silence, O God,
I am like a lonely bird
perched amidst the smoldering ruins.
I lie awake at night looking for life,
but all I see is the smoke of your wrath
and the blood vengeance
of your jealous anger.
Is this one of the many faces of your love, God,
or simply the cruel indifference
of a dark world in which I'm nothing?
What inner idolatry has called down
this fire from Heaven?
What infidelity has aroused
the smiting jealousy of your affection?

151

Jealousy you prohibit, but Jealous you are—
    shall I brand you a hypocrite,
        or weep with the depth of your love?
Inside I have tossed and turned,
    trying to climb into your mind.
Have you roosted me on this roof
    to punish me or bless me?
Either way, this perch is a solitary place,
    surrounded by a silence that swallows
the smoke-screen of words
    that threaten to separate me from you, O God.[12]
And perhaps that is the point:
    Only when the smoke has cleared
        on the naked reality of remaining things,
    will this silence of solitude
        reveal your fathomless love to me.
Till the veil falls before the Light,
    the challenge is to stare intently
        into the darkness,
looking with hungry, owl eyes
    for glimpses of your provision, God.
For the spirit must eat to stay alive;
    and the silence can either lull us to sleep,
    or heighten our awareness of things.
So the solitary places promise paradox too—
    the emptiness that feeds us,
        and the loneliness that partakes of Presence.
No man knows you, O God,
    unless, in the sanctity of silence,
his faith has found you
    quietly walking amidst his ruins.
No man has lived, O Lord,
    until he has heard you say,
"Come to me, all you who are weary
    and burdened, and I will give you rest."

[12] Thomas Merton, *Thoughts in Solitude* (New York: Farrar, Straus, and Giroux, 1999), 82.

Selected Readings for Further Study

† Ezekiel 16:1-42

† Matthew 11:25-30

Questions for Reflection and Prayer:

1. Ezekiel tells an allegory of an unfaithful Jerusalem that prostituted itself before the nations. The Lord says through the prophet, "But you [Jerusalem] trusted in your beauty and used your fame to become a prostitute"(Eze 16:15). Have you been guilty of "prostituting your beauty" to the nations? How did God respond to Jerusalem? How will He respond to you?

2. One of the many names of God is "Jealous" (Ex 34:14). Why does it matter that God is a "jealous" God? Would He truly love us if He were not jealous for our affections? What is "godly jealousy"(2 Cor 11:2)? Is there a place for it?

3. Thomas Merton says, "silence teaches us to know reality by respecting it where words have defiled it." How has God used silence in your life to teach you about "reality"? Or has your life been too "noisy" to become a pupil of God's silence?

References
        Ex 20:17; 34:14; Eze 16:1-42; Nah 1:1; Mt 11:28; 2 Cor 11:2

Diving Deeper:

1. J.D Eubanks, MD, "Lonely Places, II." in *More of Him, Less of Me* (Dawn Treader, LLC, 2018), 219.
2. Thomas Merton, *Thoughts in Solitude* (New York: Farrar, Straus, and Giroux, 1999), 81-82.

The Forty-sixth Hour

Psalm 102:8—All day long my enemies taunt me;
those who rail against me use my name as a curse.

T he way of the world
   is not your way, O Lord,
and the way of my will
   is often unwilling to go your way.
For you call us to a difficult path—
   a gauntlet of whips, sticks, and curses,
thrown out into the hatred
   of a seemingly interminable night.
Who would aspire to run this race,
   unless he meant to trade
      an eternal torment for a temporal one—
unless like Moses, turning from Egypt's treasures,
   he was looking ahead to a greater reward?
Surely this suffering has moments of simple glory,
   when the sun breaks through the clouds
      and the world is bathed in your beauty;
when in the soft landing of a butterfly
   on the velvet petals of a summer bloom,
we get glimpses of a Kingdom coming down,
   where curses give way to blessings
      and calumnies cede to benedictions.
But in the short game of here and now, Lord,
   your enemy's offer appears better—
the bread of a satisfied hunger,
   the caress of fallen angels,
      and the power and splendor of nations.
Who wouldn't want such things?
   Who but you, Lord, who in your starvation,
      rejected them all for the love of our King,
   and then went knocking at our doors,
      asking to come in and work in us the same?
Yet in this hour, I confess, my Lord,
   friendship with the world
      appears a much easier way.

154

For not only have you called me to die,
  and to keep on dying,
    day by day,
but you've asked me to *live* this dying
  amidst a crowd that loudly guffaws,
    rather than rallies.
Is this a taste of the courts of hell
  so I'm sure to spit the Liar's poison out?
And yet the taunting is almost better
  than its morbid alternative:
the cold indifference of insignificance—
  for in that mortal chill,
I might fail not only the world, but you,
  the Spirit with whom I must testify.
So let them curse, let them spit;
  let them plot, mock, and rail against me,
    as they join the chorus of hell.
Let them assign me to the grave
  as a quaint relic from another age.
For if they loved and called me their own,
  I would not be your beloved son;
and if I belonged to them, O Lord,
  I would not belong to you.
For the one who is a friend of the world
  is no friend of God's;
and the friendship of God goes only
  to the ones who are in the world,
    but not of world.
Either we are with you, Lord,
  or we are against you—
    there is no in-between.
Either we gather or we scatter;
  and the one who does not love you,
    hates you!
But who is the man who loves you, Lord?
  Is it not the one who hangs upon his cross
    as the victim of God's cruelty,
  and yet still believes this cruelty hides affection?
The man who loves you, O Lord,
  believes you do it *all* from love—
    and that man shall join the angels.[13]

---

[13] Søren Kierkegaard, *The Diary of Søren Kierkegaard* (New York: Citadel Press, 1988), 199-204.

Selected Readings for Further Study

† Psalm 59

† John 15:18-25

Questions for Reflection and Prayer:

1. Historically, some Native American tribes forced captured prisoners to "run the gauntlet." The prisoner was made to run a line between warriors and villagers armed with sticks or weapons to whip the captive. In what sense can the Christian walk be seen as a gauntlet?

2. Kierkegaard says, "Of all torments, being a Christian is the most terrible; it is—and that is how it should be—to know hell in this life." This perspective is a far cry from the warm and fuzzy, contemporary "Christian" culture of "love wins" (see Rob Bell's *Love Wins*). Is Kierkegaard a conflicted masochist, or a man who understands the true Christian faith better than most? What is the torment of Christianity?

3. Can you be a friend of the world and a friend of God at the same time? Can you claim neutrality? Abraham Heschel says, "But there is no neutrality before God; to ignore means to defy him." What does it mean to be in the world, but not of the world?

References
>   Neh 4:2; Ps 59; 69:4; Amos 5:10; Mt 5:10-12; 10:22; 12:30; Jn 15:18-25;
>   1 Cor 6:3; Heb 1:14; 11:25-26; Jas 4:4

Diving Deeper:

1. J.D. Eubanks, MD, "Likable" in *More of Him, Less of Me* (Dawn Treader, LLC, 2018), 43.
2. J.D. Eubanks, MD, "The Neutral Nothing" in *More of Him, Less of Me* (Dawn Treader, LLC, 2018), 353.
3. Søren Kierkegaard, *The Diary of Søren Kierkegaard* (New York: Citadel Press, 1988), 199-204.
4. Abraham Joshua Heschel, *Man is Not Alone* (New York: Farrar, Straus, and Giroux, 1951), 236.

156

The Forty-seventh Hour

Psalm 102:9-11—For I eat ashes as my food
and mingle my drink with tears
because of your [the Lord's] great wrath,
for you have taken me up and thrown me aside.
My days are like the evening shadow;
I wither away like grass.

O Lord, where would I be

without the thought of your wrath,
without the distant storm that builds your punch,
and the wind that threatens to carry it out?
Many times I've imagined a God
who is more than unwilling
to bring His retribution—
He is incapable:
A God who only loves me as I would be loved,
and coddles me in an unending kindness.
But would the temple of His love stand
without the pillars of justice?
Or would it be a house of cards waiting to fall
before the pursed blow masquerading as a kiss?
Does love simply give us what we want,
or does it dare to give us what we need?
Is kindness at all turns kindness,
or must love sometimes burn like fire
and bruise like the rod?
If you were a God who did not hold
the cup of your coming wrath,
would you be God at all?
For even the idol of man's love
cannot survive long without justice;
and for Love to love at all, it must be capable
of picking me up and throwing me aside.
For I fear my affection is not pure enough
to obey from love alone;

157

and if your hands did not also threaten
    to pour out your bitter wine of fury,
I might only serve you to be served by you,
    as if the crown were mine
        and the duty all yours.
You are a righteous judge, O Lord,
    a God who expresses His wrath every day.
But because of your great love,
    we are not consumed—
your fiery anger does not destroy us,
    but spits sparks into our lives
    to remind us that we—unlike you—
        can burn to ashes.
And though your zeal for your Name
    may singe us in the furnace of affliction—
though ashes may for a time be my food,
    and tears my only drink—
like the three boys in the fire,
    you have not left us all alone.
You sent your Man into the flames
    to rescue us from the coming wrath.
For your love, O Lord,
    is not the absence of fire,
    but the mercy you show in the flames.
Your grace of deliverance comes,
    not in the *from,* but the *through.*
The greatness of your Name dwells
    in the forbearance of your furnace;
and the glory you deserve only emerges
    in the refinement your forge brings.
What remains from the flames is what matters;
        for all else is dross,
    skimmed from the gold and tossed away.
And I, who am now all change,
    will at once be as unchangeable as you, God,
when at long last you decide
    to reach your great hands
        into this cauldron of cares,
    and deliver me through the flames.

† Daniel 3:1-30

† Romans 5:9-11

Questions for Reflection and Prayer:

1. Criticisms of God often include attacks on His "love." Accusers might ask:"How could a loving God allow pain and suffering in the lives of His people?" Are pain and suffering incompatible with God's love, or are they essential components of it?

2. In *The Prince*, Machiavelli argues it is better to be feared than loved. He says:

> People are less concerned with offending a man who makes himself loved than one who makes himself feared: the reason is that love is a link of obligation which men, because they are rotten, will break any time they think doing so serves their advantage; but fear involves dread of punishment, from which they can never escape.

Do you think you could obey God simply from love? Or must you also fear Him?

3. Saint Augustine says, "…if he [God] bestowed prosperity on all just for the asking we might think that God was to be served merely for the sake of those rewards, and any service of Him would prove us not godly but rather greedy and covetous." Why are you serving God? Are you serving even when He doesn't bring prosperity?

References
　　　　Dt 9:19; 29:20; 32:22; Ps 7:11; Isa 48:9; Jer 25:15; 30:23; La 2:4; 3:1; 3:22; Eze 13:13; 20:13; 33:11-11; Da 3; Hab 3:2; Ro 5:9; 9:22; 1 Thes 1:10

Diving Deeper:

1. J.D. Eubanks, MD, "Even Though" in *More of Him, Less of Me* (Dawn Treader, LLC, 2018), 308.
2. Saint Augustine, *City of God* (New York: Penguin Books, 2003), 14.
3. Niccolò Machiavelli, *The Prince* (New York: W.W. Norton &Co., 1992) 46.

The Forty-eighth Hour

Psalm 102:12—But you, O Lord, sit enthroned forever;
your renown endures through all generations.

Whether loved or hated, O Lord,

your renown is inescapable,
enduring through all generations.
Some may call it fame, others infamy—
   those cheap tricks of men
      who worship men,
and then on a whim,
   throw their heroes down
   in fickle fits of passion.
But all attention is attention,
   and whether cursed or praised,
      your Name, Lord, still sits on lips.
Only the irrelevant passes into silence;
   but you, O God, remain the same,
   yesterday, today and forever.
Your renown is that vanishing point
   from which all lines draw—
and no man builds a life in any direction,
   without reference to you.
                  ~
To all men you have given thrones,
   some great and some small,
but all for your glory, O Lord,
   in the building up or the tearing down.
The rising star of Babylon
   and the setting sun of Egypt,
      both proclaimed the same—
you raised them up to raze them down,
   that your power and glory
      might live in the memory of forever.
To be used by you or to work with you,
      O Lord, that is freedom's great choice;

and only the soul that gives
   its hidden orchestra to you, Lord,
      plays a timeless symphony—
   everything else is a resounding gong
      or a clanging cymbal.
The great man knows he is not great,
   and in his greatness
      gives his throne back to you.
But the boy holds on to fantasy,
   and with paper crown and wooden scepter,
      tells himself it's all real.
Even the mirror of truth fails to capture him,
   and when he turns,
      he is still convinced he is King.
But games don't last forever,
   and better to be the boy broken early
      than the would-be king too late.
For no one escapes the Name
   above every other name,
and at the name of Jesus
   every knee shall bow,
      in Heaven, on earth and under earth,
and every tongue confess
   to the renown of the Ancient of Days.

                    ~

Blessed is the man, O Lord,
   who walks in the way of your laws,
the one you guide in paths of righteousness
   for your name's sake.
Your Name and renown, Lord,
      are the desire of his heart,
   and his glory is to glory in the Glory.
But though your grace falls upon the wicked,
   they do not learn your righteousness;
though all they have is from you, Lord,
   they do not see your hand lifted high.
But the man of God is known by God,
   and he knows God's glory lies
      in His limitless love to him.

161

Selected Readings for Further Study

† Isaiah 63:11-19

† Philippians 2:9-11

Questions for Reflection and Prayer:

1. The Lord tells His people He will "not hold anyone guiltless who misuses His name"(Ex 20:7). Why does God care so much for the *renown* His name? Why should you?

2. In Acts, the Apostles preach, baptize, forgive sins, resurrect the dead, and drive out demons—all in the *name of Jesus*. Have you considered the power of Jesus' name for your life? What will the *name of Jesus* bring when He comes again?

3. In one of his early works, Albert Camus says, "Here I understand what is meant by glory: the right to love without limits." If Camus is correct, can anyone but God truly claim glory? Has anyone but Christ ever loved without limits?

References

  Ex 9:16; 20:7; Ps 23:13; 25:11; 31:3; 135:13; Isa 26:7-11; 55:13; 63:11-19; Jer 13:11; Eze 20:44; 26:17; Php 2:9-11; Heb 13:8

Diving Deeper:

1. J.D. Eubanks, MD, "Symphony of the Soul" in *More of Him, Less of Me* (Dawn Treader, LLC, 2018), 169.
2. G.K. Chesterton, *The Everlasting Man* (Oxford, England: Oxford City Press, 2011), 159.
3. Albert Camus, "Nuptials at Tipasa" in *Personal Writings* (New York: Vintage International, 2020), 73.

The Forty-ninth Hour

At times, O Lord,

time is a friend of the heart;
at times it is the fiercest enemy
of our hopes.
Sometimes time travels like light;
sometimes it creeps as it carves
with heavy glacial force.
There are times when time heals,
and times when it seems to be killing us,
even as we have tried to kill time.
Time is the torrent you use, Lord,
to shape the landscape of the soul.
And there is a time for everything,
and a season for every activity under Heaven.
But at all times, time belongs to you, God;
and time is not time,
unless it is appointed by your will.
Neither a sparrow falls from the sky
before you say it should,
nor does a star go black into the black,
till the second you have set.
All the days you have ordained for me
were determined before I began;
and what began in a brilliant big bang,
will one day end
in a curtain that rises to you.
For the time of the end
will come at its appointed time,

163

and only you, the Father of our hours,
   know when that moment will come.
Even the angels at your side, Lord,
   long to look into these things,
waiting as they are with eager expectation
   for the day when time
      will finally be timeless.
The demons know it too,
   and the powers of darkness shiver
      to think on the hour of their demise.
For the revelation awaits an appointed time;
   it speaks of the end
   and will not prove false.
And though it lingers, we wait for it;
   it will certainly come and will not delay.
A blinding light will fill the darkness,
   and what was once hidden
      will at last be exposed.
The heavenly gavel will finally fall, Lord,
   to crown some in your glory
      and hurtle others into your fire.
These visions of the end
   await their appointed time,
flying in distant circles
   until you clear them to land.
For even you, Maker of the hours—
   for whom one day is like a thousand,
   and thousand like one—
patiently waited on the ripened hour
   to unveil your ministry to men.
You, O Lord, who existed before time,
   chose to step into the river
      running from you,
so that for a brief—soon closing moment—
   the water would wall up
   to reveal the path to your promise.
And though the river keeps running,
   the stones still stand
      for faithful eyes to follow.

<u>Selected Readings for Further Study</u>

† Joshua 4:1-24

† 1 Corinthians 4:1-5

<u>Questions for Reflection and Prayer:</u>

1. Like the inescapable nature of gravity, time is one of the universe's fundamental "forces." No moment of our lives is not touched by time. And because no life on earth escapes time, God often uses it to do His work in our lives. How has God used time in your life to shape your faith?

2. The Bible often uses the term "appointed time." God had appointed times for rituals, sacrifices, the revelation of prophecies, and the emergence of His own ministry on earth. But all of these anticipate one final "appointed time." How can the knowledge of God's appointment of time change the way you live today?

3. The Stoic philosopher, Marcus Aurelius, says, "Time is a river, a violent current of events, glimpsed once and already carried past us, and another follows and is gone." The Greek philosopher, Heraclitus, sees man in that river: "No man ever steps in the same river twice, for it's not the same river and he's not the same man." In anticipation of the final "appointed time," every minute in the river matters—for it is never the same river, and I'm never the same man. Unless, of course, God steps into that river. When God steps into the Jordan to hold back the water, we—like the Israelites—must be ready to cross over to the Promised Land. Are you ready?

References
> Jos 4:1-24; Ps 75:2; Da 8:19; 11:27; 29; 35; Hab 2:3; Mt 8:29; 26:18;
> Lk 1:20; 1 Cor 4:1-5; 2 Tim 1:9; Titus 1:2; 2 Pe 3:8;

<u>Diving Deeper:</u>

1. J.D. Eubanks, MD, "Time" in *More of Him, Less of Me* (Dawn Treader, LLC, 2018), 334.
2. J.D. Eubanks, MD, "Perfect Timing" in *More of Him, Less of Me* (Dawn Treader, LLC, 2018), 97.
3. Marcus Aurelius, *Meditations* (Public Domain).

165

The Fiftieth Hour

Psalm 102:15—The nations will fear the Name of the Lord,
all the kings of the earth will revere your glory.

Y ou are the Lord of Hosts, O God,

who thunders at the head of His army;
because of the countless feet
that march under your banner, I fear you!
You are the Maker of Heaven and earth, Lord,
and I am a grain of sand
on one small beach,
bowed before your endless expanse—
I have been made in your pounding waves.
You are the Judge for the coming trial.
Who can fail to tremble
at your balanced scale of justice and love?
You are the Father who embraces me,
and the Brother who is my constant advocate—
how can I not quiver in your arms?
For what is man, that you care for him,
the son of man, that you consider him?
And if you consider him, Lord,
how can he not consider you?
How can a love-sick child be held
without feeling the arms around him?
Who is the man who can look into the stars
and fail to wonder at your works, O Lord;
who dares to see in your finest details,
the bleak indifference of meaninglessness;
and in that dark void, a defiant comfort
in his bold bracing before
the cold air of chance?
There is far too much meaning
in the meaning of things,
for there to be no Meaning.

166

And the man who beats his breast
  declaring himself free of you, Lord,
    is merely the prisoner of a host of demons.
He lives in the web of his own fears—
  chased by plagues, haunted by downturns,
    stalked by loneliness and hounded by opinion.
There is no end to his worries;
  they are a ceaseless spiral of anxieties
    catching his would-be wings.
As soon as he frees himself from one ring,
  he is caught in another—
    his desperate struggle for freedom
  only hastens his creeping death.
For the one who does not fear you, O God,
  lives in fear of everything else;
but the man who fears the Lord
  need never fear again.
Though the earth give way
  and mountains fall into the sea;
though pestilence stalks in the darkness,
  and a thousand fall at his side,
    the one who fears the Lord
  shall not fear the fears of men.
For holy fear drowns all other fears,
  and the one who fears you, O Lord,
    floats on fears by the buoyancy of your love.
Your servant will be carried by the vessel
    of your unending affection
  toward the sanctuary you have made,
until you set him down upon the mountain,
  to look out on the world
      you have reclaimed
  in your violent goodness.
Then the nations will walk in your light,
  and the kings will bring their glory to you.
There will be no more night and no more fear,
  for those who lived fearing you, Lord;
for the light of your love will swallow their darkness,
  and only glory will remain.

† Isaiah 8:11-22

† Revelation 21:24-27

Questions for Reflection and Prayer:

1. God tells us to "fear" Him (Isa 8:11-14). What does He mean by this? How is a fear of God different from other fears? Why does God want us to fear Him?

2. Blaise Pascal divides fear into two categories:

> True fear comes from faith; false fear comes from doubt. True fear is joined to hope, because it is born of faith, and because men hope in the God in whom they believe. False fear is joined to despair, because men fear in the God in whom they have no belief. The former fear to lose Him; the latter fear to find Him.

False fear threatens to touch every category of our lives. It plagues men who fear to find God. But true fear is rooted in faith and hope. It is a holy fear that frees. Have you found this freedom, or are you still caught in the web of your anxieties?

3. The Apostle John says there is no fear in love (1 Jn 4:18). If we are called to fear God—and by definition, God is love—how can there be no fear in love? What does the Apostle mean? How does holy fear both generate love and emanate from Love? Can we truly love the Lord without "fearing" Him?

References
> Ps 8:4; 46:2-3; 72:11,17; 91; 112:1, 6-8; Isa 8:11-14; 41:10; Joel 2:11; 1 Jn 4:18; Rev 21:24-27

Diving Deeper:

1. J.D. Eubanks, MD, "Anxiety" in *More of Him, Less of Me* (Dawn Treader, LLC, 2018), 203.
2. Blaise Pascal, *Pensées* (New York: Random House, Inc., 1941), 92.

The Fifty-first Hour

Psalm 102:16—For the Lord will rebuild Zion,
and appear in His glory.

W ho among the gods is like you, O Lord?

Who is like you—
    majestic in holiness,
    awesome in glory,
    working wonders?
You are the King of glory,
    and only the heavens never fail
        to ascribe to your Name
    the glory you are due.
Day after day, the stars burn for you—
    when I consider their constant praise,
        I am amazed; I am ashamed.
For in this hour I confess, O Lord,
    I have often neglected your praise.
Somewhere in the ceaseless slog,
    my wonder has grown old.
That eternal appetite of infancy[14]
    you stitched into our souls,
has been curbed by comforts
    and deadened by difficulties.
The muck that sticks to my every step
    draws my wide eyes from you to me;
and where I should be a happy child
    simply staring into your face,
    perhaps I have grown older than God.
At times I have even dared
    to climb your holy mountain
        and claim your fire as my own,
    as if glory could exist without you.

---

[14] G.K. Chesterton, *Orthodoxy* (Peabody, MA: Hendrickson Publishers, 2006), 55.

169

But the fullness of your glory
  will not dwell again in a man
    until you return to Zion.
Then the vessels you've created for your glory
  will finally shine like stars in the universe.
For you, Lord, will be the everlasting light
  shining through your chosen ones,
and those who have persevered in righteousness—
  who have sought in you
    glory, honor, and immortality—
  will finally claim the priceless pearl.
This is the promise of glory—
  to stand before the King,
    dressed as the King;
to become, by some stroke of magic,
  the Father's ultimate delight.
It is a weight of glory no man can bear,
  until you, Lord, bear our burdens for us.
For apart from *you*, I am Ichabod;
  but in *you*, I am Christ.
Without *you*, I am a child of darkness;
  but in *you*, I am the Light of the world.
And the Son who has come,
  will come again in glory,
    to raise us up into His light.
Then we will walk streets of gold
  with our heads held high;
then we shall be crowned
  in a glory that never fades—
  dressed in a radiance that never dims.
Then we shall see you, O Lord,
  face to face,
    as you move the moon
  to reveal your Sun,
and the God I once knew
  in the thin penumbra
    of a dark world,
will show me a glory
  no wonder will ever satisfy.

Selected Readings for Further Study

† 1 Samuel 4:1-22

† 2 Corinthians 3:7-18

Questions for Reflection and Prayer:

1. Theologian Abraham Heschel recognizes the importance of *wonder* in our lives: "The beginning of our happiness lies in the understanding that life without wonder is not worth living." Chesterton couldn't agree more. He stresses the need for the "eternal appetite of infancy," for he says, "we have sinned and grown old, and our Father is younger than we." Have you stifled your "eternal appetite of infancy"? Have you allowed yourself to grow older than God?

2. The name, Ichabod, means "no glory." When the ark is captured by the Philistines, Samuel's dying daughter-in-law aptly names his grandson, Ichabod. The ark was the Presence of God's glory amidst His people. When the ark left, the glory left. Have you turned God's glory into shame in your life (Ps 4:2; Hab 2:16)?

3. C.S. Lewis says, "To please God...to be loved by God, not merely pitied, but delighted in as an artist delights in his work or a father in a son—it seems impossible, a weight or burden of glory which our thoughts can hardly sustain. But it is so." God is glory. And when God lives in us, His glory dwells in us. Have you considered your wonderful weight of glory? What does it mean for your life?

References
      Ex 15:4; Lev 26:13; Dt 5:24; 1 Sam 5:21-22; Ps 4:2; 19:1; 24; 29; Isa 42:8; 43:7; 60:19; Hab 2:16; Ro 2:7; 8:17; 2 Cor 3:11-18; Heb 1:3; 1 Pe 5:1,4,10

Diving Deeper:

1. J.D. Eubanks, MD, "Penumbra" in *More of Him, Less of Me* (Dawn Treader, LLC, 2018), 357.
2. Abraham Joshua Heschel, *Man is Not Alone* (New York: Farrar, Straus, Giroux, 1951), 37.
3. C.S. Lewis, *The Weight of Glory* (New York: HarperOne, 2001), 39.

Psalm 102:17—He [God] will respond to the prayer of the destitute;
He will not despise their plea.

W here is the border, O Lord,

between destitution and death,
between the rock-bottom depths
    that drown us,
and the soul-sick poverty
    that pushes us to splendor?
No man knows his limit
    until he is pushed to it;
until, by blood, sweat and tears,
    he ascends the horizon's highest hill,
only to find that it is the first of many,
    and the coming climbs
        stretch out before him,
    like endless waves of the sea.
Only heroes survive this journey—
    wandering in deserts and mountains,
    sheltering in caves and holes—
        the world is not worthy of them.
But I am not a champion, O Lord,
    just a fallen man
    with a body breaking down before me,
        and a heart wearied to barely a beat.
Guilty men may have strength as their god;
    but even if I wanted to bow
        before this brazen demon,
    I have no strength left to worship.
I lift my eyes to the hills—
    where does my help come from?
Will you, Lord, be the one to give me
    the courage I do not have
        and the hope I no longer possess?

172

Are you the Sovereign of my strength,
    the Lord who can make my feet
        like the feet of the deer
    and enable me to go on the heights?
The ancients found life in faith,
    and though chained, stoned,
        and sawed in two, somehow, Lord,
    they hung on to your rocky grace.
And we remember their names,
    not for what they obtained,
        but for what they endured.
For none of them received
    what was promised,
and all of them are still waiting
    until their perfection comes with ours.
From first breath to death,
    life is a constant struggle,
an endless grapple with what we want
        and what is,
    both without and within.
Wrestling with pain and sorrow,
    I have wrestled in prayer before you, Lord.
In my penury, I have never dared hope
    to please you with my pleas,
        only to catch the careless pennies
    you toss my way.
For you have promised to hear
    the prayer of the righteous;
and though there is no one righteous,
    the unrighteous stand righteous in you.
Therefore, I hazard to hope, O God,
    you will see through me to you;
and in the radiance of your Son's face,
    you will hear from Heaven
        my prayer and plea—
you will forgive and act;
    you will uphold my cause.
For the Lord is my strength and shield;
    my heart trusts in Him, and He helps me.

173

Selected Readings for Further Study

† 1 Kings 8:22-53

† Hebrews 11:32-40

Questions for Reflection and Prayer:

1. Andrew Murray describes the battle for prayer: "Now how does Satan hinder prayer? By temptation to postpone or curtail it, by bringing in wandering thoughts and all sorts of distractions, or through unbelief and hopelessness." Which of these three categories most hinders your prayer life?

2. The victories of faith celebrated in Hebrews 11 were preceded by prayer. Murray says, "Happy is the prayer hero who, through it all, takes care to hold fast and use his weapon [prayer]. Like our Lord in Gethsemane, the more violently the Enemy attacked, the more earnestly He prayed and did not cease until He obtained the victory."

So much of the Christian journey is about "holding on"—about wrestling with the enemy as we wrestle in prayer (Col 4:12). As Murray points out, the "hero" holds on in prayer like Christ in Gethsemane. But what do you do when you are not capable of heroism? Where do you turn when you feel too exhausted to pray?

3. The writer of Hebrews tells us the "heroes" of faith did *not* "receive what was promised." Like Moses on Pisgah, they only viewed it from a distance. And yet, they held on in faith. Can this be an encouragement to you in your discouragement?

References
        1 Ki 8:22-53; Ps 28:7; 121:1; Pr 15:8, 29; Isa 26:16; 38:5; Hab 1:11; 3:19;
        Ro 3:10; Php 4:6; Col 4:12; 1 Pe 3:12

Diving Deeper:

1. J.D. Eubanks, MD, "Only by Prayer" in *More of Him, Less of Me* (Dawn Treader, LLC, 2018), 361.
2. Andrew Murray, *The Prayer Life* in *Collected Works on Prayer* (New Kensington, PA: Whitaker House, 2013), 221.

The Fifty-third Hour

Psalm 102:18-20—Let this be written for a future generation,
that a people not yet created may praise the Lord:
"The Lord looked down from His sanctuary on high,
from Heaven He viewed the earth,
to hear the groans of the prisoners
and release those condemned to death."

U p and down

is to down and out,
as Heaven and earth
are to man in the middle
of his endless muddle.
For from your sanctuary, O God,
everything is below,
and there is no heart—
much less mine—
that has never longed
from little things to look up.
But what a ladder lies between us!—
the Prince and this pauper—
with rungs that outnumber the stars,
and slippery rails that run gleaming
from the muck to the mansion.
Your house is on high,
perched between cloudy clefts,
a palace of many rooms.
And you have gone
from there to here and back again,
to prepare a place for me?
In this dark hour it seems too much,
a fantasy for the enfeebled
who have dared to believe,
that when you look down
you give us cause to look up.

175

Pity has never been enough for you, Lord;
   and compassion that does not dive in,
     a divine counterfeit.
For when you cast your gaze
   into the gutters, Lord,
it was to find footing for your feet,
   and the fitting flesh
     for your divine commiseration.
You took on ears and hands,
   to hear the groans of the prisoners,
   to bind up the brokenhearted,
     and release the captives.
You stooped down to make me great,
   as your greatness bound itself
     in the gentleness of a baby.
Your first cry changed the world,
   for now that God was in a man,
     man might forever be in God.
But all who forsake you, Lord,
   the Hope of Israel,
   will be put to shame.
Those who turn away from you
   will be written in the dust.
And only you can tell us
   what you wrote in the dirt,
   kneeling before the one they despised.
For the hands full of stones,
   thinking they were right, had it all wrong;
and in looking down into the dust, Lord,
   you chose to raise her up.
This is the journey you take,
   time and time again—
     the silence of salvation
in the forward bend with a basin,
   and the gentle reach
   for the road-weary feet.
To do as you have done for me, Lord—
   can the feet of a man
     ever fill such shoes?

Selected Readings for Further Study

† Isaiah 61:1-3

† John 8:1-11

Questions for Reflection and Prayer:

1. An old Scottish proverb says, "Many a little makes a mickle." Later, it became corrupted and morphed into, "Many a mickle makes a muckle." In either iteration, it means: Many little things add up to a big thing. If God lives "on high," how can He care about the messy mickles of our muddled lives? How has He definitively shown us He does care?

2. When Jesus knelt to write in the dirt, theologian Kenneth Bailey is "convinced that he wrote, 'death' or 'kill her' or 'stone her with stones.' His following words presuppose that he decreed the death penalty." If Bailey is correct, why do you think Christ then orchestrated the public forgiveness of the woman caught in adultery? Have you ever been this woman? Have you ever held the stones?

3.The late philosopher, Anne Dufourmantelle, notes something special about the Incarnation. She says, "Placing spiritual royalty in the place of the greatest vulnerability was a coup de force unprecedented in History. All the values of merit, of power, and of military prowess found themselves disrupted." In short: the Incarnation was a miracle on many levels. It was revolutionary. It was Omnipotence taking on nothingness. What does this miracle mean for you?

References
Isa 61:1-3; Jer 17:13; Lk 4:14-30; Jn 8:1-11; 14:1-4

Diving Deeper:

1. J.D. Eubanks, MD, "Jesus Came Down" in *More of Him, Less of Me* (Dawn Treader, LLC, 2018), 11.
2. Kenneth E. Bailey, *Jesus Through Middle Eastern Eyes* (Downers Grove, IL: InterVarsity Press, 2008), 235.
3. Anne Dufourmantelle, *Power of Gentleness: Meditations on the Risk of Living* (New York: Fordham University Press, 2018), 28-29.

Psalm 102:21-22—So the Name of the Lord will be declared in Zion
and His praise in Jerusalem
when the peoples and the kingdoms
assemble to worship the Lord.

The day of your coming

is coming, O Lord,
  like a thief in the night
it approaches the world's slumber.
Many a man will still be lost
  in the sweet horror of his dreams,
    lulled by the siren song of fantasy,
when the heavens disappear
  with a cosmic roar,
and the earth is laid bare,
  stripped of her false finery
    like a whore no more.
Fire, fire everywhere!
  Flames for the fierce spirits
    who have trampled your Holy Name, Lord.
Then we shall see it—
  your Name written on the ones you love,
    never to be cast down again.
Then the city shall descend,
  dressed as a radiant bride
    softly laid down
  in the arms of a new heaven and earth.
And the name of that city will be:
  THE LORD IS THERE.
For you shall be in your city,
  never to leave it again.
The roar that swallowed the darkness
  will give way to a loud voice declaring,
    "Now the dwelling of God is with men,
      and He will live with them.

They will be His people, and God Himself
will be with them and be their God."
And the nations will come,
   from the far corners of the earth
      they will flock to the Holy City.
The great horde that once followed
   the cloud and the flame,
      will be as nothing
   compared to this righteous caravan.
For from all peoples they will draw,
   knowing few, sharing less,
      but all in love
   with the King who calls their names.
But on that day, Lord,
   only one name will be on our lips.
At that Name, every knee will bow
   and every tongue confess,
      Jesus Christ is Lord!
Your praise will roll like thunder
   from my lips, O God,
and I will join the multitudes
   who flock to the mountain of the Lord,
wanting to know only your ways,
   desiring to walk in nothing
      but your paths.
The sword shall become a plowshare,
   the spear a pruning hook,
and the tongue an instrument,
   no longer of death and destruction,
      but praise and adoration.
For your Name, O Lord,
   will be on the tip of my tongue;
and the song I now sing,
   in its pitiful spits and spurts,
will finally be redeemed
   for a paean of unending praise!

<u>Selected Readings for Further Study</u>

† Isaiah 2:1-5

† 2 Peter 3:10-13

<u>Questions for Reflection and Prayer:</u>

1. As the Apostle Peter describes it, "The Day of the Lord" will be both *horrific* and *fantastic* at the same time. The "fantastic," however, will only be claimed by those who "live holy and godly lives as [they] look forward to the day of God and speed its coming"(2 Pe 3:11-12). Are you living a life of grace capable of claiming the "fantastic" future?

2. When we consider the coming flames, some of us might cringe in horror for those we know who have rejected God. But as theologian Jerry Walls reminds us, "if hell is freely chosen by sinners who are given every opportunity to repent, but who persistently refuse the offer of grace, it is at least clear that they have chosen their own lot." What lot have you chosen? Are you praying for those who have yet to repent?

3. Heaven promises to be a place of singing (Rev 5:8-14). Are you preparing your voice for eternity? What "singing exercises" of the soul are you planning to do today? How can you better tune your voice for eternity?

References
    Isa 2:1-5; Eze 48:35; Zec 14:9; 2 Pe 3:10-13; Rev 3:12; 5:8-14; 21:1-4, 10

<u>Diving Deeper:</u>

1. J.D. Eubanks, MD, "On the Heels of Singing" in *More of Him, Less of Me* (Dawn Treader, LLC, 2018), 356.
2. Denny Burk, John Stackhouse, Jr., Robin Parry, and Jerry Walls, *Four Views of Hell* (Grand Rapids, MI: Zondervan, 2016), 80.

The Fifty-fifth Hour

Psalm 102:23-24—In the course of my life He [God] broke my strength;
He cut short my days.
So I said:
"Do not take me away, O my God, in the
midst of my days;
your years go on through all generations."

B roken, your world is broken, Lord,

broken in the main, broken in the man.
The breaking began in the Garden—
one question to shatter commitment
to your only command.
And the reach for the fruit-laden bough
set the soul's dominoes
forever falling—
the devil dealt his master blow.
But what if, in ignorance, Eve had picked
the ripened fruit of the other tree?
What if she had not reached for knowledge—
for the brokenness of good and evil—
but for the wholeness of life?
For it too was there for the taking,
the sweetness of the tree
whose roots drink deeply
from the crystal water
flowing down from the throne.
If she might have reached for knowledge,
she might have reached for life.
But freedom's choice is so often
a world of hurt,
and when the Liar leans into us,
a spiral of pain may spin us
in directions we've never imagined—

kicked out of Eden, subject to death;
  a slave of the soil and a servant of suffering.
O Lord, you could have stopped her,
  but you didn't.
You could keep your hammer
  from smashing my dreams to bits,
    but you haven't.
So wholeness must depend on brokenness,
  as life depends upon death.
And to have tasted of life too early,
  might have forgone
    our chance for future glory.
For if we were gods from the beginning,
  we might have been forever lost
    in our illusions of self-sufficiency.
The reach for true glory
  comes only from the grave,
and a man will never seek to be healed,
  until his disease
    is beyond his own curing.
The leaves of your great tree, Lord,
  are for healing the nations;
yet if the curse had not come,
  we would not need
    a balm for our brokenness.
It would all seem a cruel, protracted joke,
  but for the fact that you entered in, Lord—
you put your skin in the game,
  and became the bread of life
  that broke itself for the broken,
that they, in partaking of your brokenness,
  might themselves become
    the broken bread
  given to a starving world.
Your glory, O God,
  has always been in the giving;
and no man will join you in your joy,
  until he too is broken into pieces,
    given to the world in your Name.

† Genesis 3:1-7

† Revelation 22:1-5

Questions for Reflection and Prayer:

1. The biblical metanarrative hinges on the word "broken." It begins with the breaking of God's single command in the Garden of Eden and then moves into the heart—like that of the devil's who incited it all—which sins defiantly (Nu 15:30-31). Not by mistake, however, the antidote to this curse is brokenness itself—Christ who broke Himself for us, breaking the curse of sin—and then the brokenness in us that leads us to repentance. Have you been broken?

2. C.S. Lewis says, "The creature's illusion of self-sufficiency must, for the creature's sake, be shattered; and…God shatters it 'unmindful of His glory's diminution'." What do you think would have happened if Eve ate from the tree of life instead of the tree of knowledge? Do you think we could have ever hoped to be free of our "illusion of self-sufficiency"?

3. Henri Nouwen reminds us: As disciples of Jesus we are "chosen, blessed and broken so as to be given." Christ broke Himself to give Himself to us. And then He says to us, "Go and do as I have done for you." Have you become broken bread given to the world?

References
    Ge 3:1-7; Ps 51:17; Mt 26:26-29; Jn 6:35-40; Rev 22:1-5

Diving Deeper:

1. J.D. Eubanks, MD, "The Giver and the Given" in *More of Him, Less of Me* (Dawn Treader, LLC, 2018), 333.
2. C.S. Lewis, *The Problem of Pain* (New York: HarperCollins, 1996), 96.
3. Henri Nouwen, *Life of the Beloved* (New York: The CrossRoad Publishing Company, 2002), 121.

The Fifty-sixth Hour

Psalm 102:25—In the beginning you [God] laid the foundations of the earth, and the heavens are the work of your hands.

O Lord, what is a tiny blue planet

floating in an endless sea of stars?
To consider earth is to consider man;
   and to stand in the stellar dust
      from which I am made,
peering into the deep heavens
      from where I have come,
         is to feel all at once
      both loved and lost.
The whole thing is absurd really,
   a complex matter of matter,
      and a fine string
      of infinite "coincidences"
placing a thinking, feeling man
   on a peaceful rock
      in a hostile universe.
This is fantasy at its finest,
   a story too incredible to be real.
But then it keeps on going,
   measure after measure
      of nature's fine-tuning,
to play a singular symphony
   unmatched in an ocean of galaxies.
Your enemies, O Lord,
   want to see it all without you—
not as the gift of God,
   but of Goldilocks,
and an uncountable series of chances,
   perfectly ordered
      to bring calm to chaos
      and elegant equations to enormity.

From beginning to a distant end,
  your adversaries weave theories
  to write you out of your work, O God.
But then there is that beginning,
  which even the wisest of them
    cannot explain:
the primeval atom that birthed
  brilliance into being—
    Where did it come from?
  What does it mean?
Long ago, before we looked
  into these deep things,
the sorcerers saw it all—
  the finger of God.
For what is the absurd—
  that I am a man in the multitude,
  claiming a passing second of eternity
in a lonely universe
  that coughed me up
    only to swallow me again?
Or is it the truth
  that gnaws at reason,
and claims there is a God
  who lives in the land
  beyond neat explanations;
a God whose hand worked it all
  from blueprint to beauty,
so He might enter into time,
  a willing subject of His of subjects,
    to reclaim it all
in a lonely, agonizing cry?
Each man must pick his poison,
  for his conscience cannot lie;
and though his reason lives
  in finite realms,
    his spirit must answer the Infinite.
O Lord, I reach for your cup—
  now give me the grace to drink it down,
  till meaning comes to madness.

Selected Readings for Further Study

† Exodus 8:1-19

† Colossians 1:15-23

Questions for Reflection and Prayer:

1. In his book, *Is Atheism Dead?*, Eric Metaxas quotes astrophysicist, Hugh Ross:

> [the] degree of fine-tuning [in the universe] is so great that it's as if right after the universe's beginning someone could have destroyed the possibility of life within it by subtracting a single dime's mass from the whole of the observable universe or adding a single dime's mass to it.

When you consider the universe, have you considered its "fine-tuning"? A single dime's mass, less or more, and nothing exists. Is this chance or the finger of God?

2. Albert Camus says, "This world in itself is not reasonable, that is all that can be said." How have you dealt with this confrontation with the "unreasonable"?

3. Kierkegaard lionizes Abraham as a man who—through an act of faith—embraces "the strength of the absurd" in the face of the absurdity in which he lived. Have you dealt with the absurdity of your existence? What does Scripture have to say?

References
    Ex 8:1-19; Ps 8:3-4; Mt 27:45-46; Lk 23:44-46; Col 1:15-16; Heb 1:1-2

Diving Deeper:

1. J.D. Eubanks, MD, "The Singularity" in *More of Him, Less of Me* (Dawn Treader, LLC, 2018), 367.
2. Eric Metaxas, *Is Atheism Dead?* (Washington, D.C., Salem Books, 2021), 60.
3. Albert Camus, *The Myth of Sisyphus* (New York: Vintage International, 1991), 21.
4. Søren Kierkegaard, *Fear and Trembling* (New York: Penguin Books, 2003), 65-67.

The Fifty-seventh Hour

Psalm 102:26—"They [the heavens and the earth] will perish,
but you [God] remain.
They will wear out like a garment.
Like clothing you will change them
and they will be discarded."

O Lord, nothing that is
  will forever be,
and what is here today,
  will be gone tomorrow.
Even the fixed constants
  of Heaven and earth,
will one day wear out
  like a well-loved garment
    beyond the point
  of patching.
For you have dressed the world
  in a tragic splendor, God,
wrapping the planet in blue garments
  of water and air
that give the earth
  what only you can—
    life and breath passing
within a fragile, glass-like globe,
  waiting to be shattered
    in a dark, hungry sea.
But even this miracle
  was not enough for you, Lord,
till you dared to spread
  the corner of your robe
    over the lover at your feet,
promising her a covenant of covering
  in the violent and inconstant world,
    gone from good to blighted.

But where the Moabitess prevailed,
   your people failed;
for one humbly sought
   the corner of her redeemer's garment,
while the other threw off His gift
   at the foot of high places.
One became the mother of kings,
   while the other was stripped naked,
      stoned, and hacked to pieces.
What we become depends upon
      what we do
   with the garments you give us, Lord.
For though you have dressed us
      with a splendor
   that makes our beauty glorious,
you have also granted us the freedom
   to trust in the beauty you have given—
      to throw our jewels and garments down
   before the idols we have made.
Yet idols fall with heads that roll,
   and the temples of our affections
      will crumble to rubble
   before the jealous wrath
      of the Lover we have despised.
And the rich garments
   you have wrapped around us, God,
will lie limp at our feet,
   like the silent mounds of the dead—
      buried ships on a voyage to nowhere.
For only the one who wraps herself
      in your right, Lord,
   who guards your imperishable
      Word in her heart,
will stand under heavens on fire
      to trade her ashes
   for a crown of beauty,
and her spirit of despair,
   for the garment of praise
      woven with your light.

Selected Readings for Further Study

† Isaiah 51:4-8

† Matthew 5:18; 24:32-51

Questions for Reflection and Prayer:

1. The story of Ruth at the feet of her kinsman-redeemer, Boaz, has something to teach every one of us (Ruth 3). How does Ruth approach her redeemer? What is her request? How have you approached your Redeemer? Have you asked Him to spread His garment over you?

2. Jesus says, "Heaven and earth will pass away, but my words will never pass away." What does He mean by Heaven and earth passing away? When He creates a "new heaven and a new earth," will they resemble the current ones, albeit perfected?

3. In his book, *Surprised by Hope*, theologian N.T. Wright argues that the "recreation of God's wonderful world…began with the resurrection of Jesus and continues mysteriously as God's people live in the risen Christ and in the power of the Spirit…." If Wright is correct, how does his interpretation jibe with the multiple scriptural passages describing the coming "destruction" and "passing" of Heaven and earth? Are we part of an ongoing redemption process, prefigured in the risen Christ; or, will God one day destroy what we now know in order to create something entirely new? Is the "recreation" Wright intimates more of an inward one in God's disciples, distinct from what Christ's coming will bring to earth?

References
> Ru 3:9; Job 38: 9, 14; Ps 104:2, 6; Isa 51:6; 61:3; 65:17; Eze 16:8, 16;
> Mt 5:18; 24:35; Lk 5:36; Heb 12:27; 2 Pe 3:10, 13; 1 Jn 2:17; Rev 21:1-27

Diving Deeper:

1. J.D. Eubanks, MD, "Inward Renewal" in *More of Him, Less of Me* (Dawn Treader, LLC, 2018), 129.
2. N.T. Wright, *Surprised by Hope: Rethinking Heaven, the Resurrection, and the Mission of the Church* (New York: HarperOne, 2008), 208.

Psalm 102:27-28—"But you [Lord] remain the same,
and your years will never end.
The children of your servants will live
in your Presence;
their descendants will be established before you."

Almighty Father,

you are the God of descendants,
the Lord who presides
over all the generations.
From the first seed,
till the last withering bloom,
you are the God
who was, and is,
and is to come—
the Lord who never changes,
and the God who remains
ageless in the ages.
You are the Great Tragedian
whose scripts are fathomless
tales of sorrowful beauty,
stretched out over generations
that simply come and go.
Some players have found your favor,
with big scenes and bold promises.
Their names have survived
in the pages of time,
and their descendants have numbered
with the stars in the sky
and the sand on the shore.
But most of us are only actors as extras,
who have dressed for bit parts,
lost in the background
and a list of credits
no one—but you, God?—reads.

It would all seem meaningless,
   utterly meaningless, Lord,
except that you know my name,
   and you have summoned me
      onto this grim stage
      to declare me as your own.
Like a shepherd you have called me;
   by name you have led me out
   from the prison of my pen.
The timbre of your voice leads me
   through the darkness
      to a distant pasture
      I sense, but cannot see.
You are the Good Shepherd,
   who for the love of His sheep—
      even one as lost as me—
   became a lamb to save the flock.
You were led to the slaughter, Lord,
   a sheep in the jaws of a wolf
      who came—and still comes—for me.
And who can count your descendants?
   Did you become the father of children
      who sat on your lap
   and smiled into your face?
Was yours the simple joy of fatherhood,
   or the dread duty of a man of sorrows
      for a people of sorrow,
so that in the greatest twist of plot
   the world has ever known,
your script might transform
   tragedy into triumph,
to lead your true children
   through your narrow gate
   into the Kingdom's broad spaces?
For there, in fields of glory,
   you will call me by the name
      you have never forgotten,
   and I will come,
      running for my Redeemer.

Selected Readings for Further Study

† Isaiah 43:1; 48:18-19; 53:7-8

† John 10:1-18

Questions for Reflection and Prayer:

1. In Shakespeare's *As You Like It*, Jaques says, "All the world's a stage,/ And all men and women merely players./ They have their exits and their entrances...." As Shakespeare points out, there is a sense in which all our lives are part of an epic play; we are all playing out our parts. What part are you playing in God's script? Are you playing it well? For as Stoic philosopher Epictetus says, "Although we can't control which roles are assigned to us, it must be our business to act our given role as best as we possibly can and to refrain from complaining about it."

2. Men like Abraham and David were prime actors in God's drama. They were given great promises for their lives and for their innumerable descendants. But the greatest character in the divine drama—Jesus—was a man with no direct biologic descendants (Isa 53:8). And yet, His spiritual descendants outnumber the stars. What lesson is there for us in Christ's example?

3. One of the greatest comforts Christianity brings is the promise that Christ knows our names. He is the Good Shepherd who never forgets a single one of His sheep, no matter how small they are or how large the flock they find themselves in. Even though your part in God's drama may seem small, have you considered that He knows your name and His voice is calling you even now?

References
Ge 17:7; 22:17; 28:14; Ps 139:1-6; Ecc 1:1, 11; Isa 43:1; 48:18-19: 53:7-8; Jn 10:1-18; Acts 8:33

Diving Deeper:

1. J.D. Eubanks, MD, "The Good Shepherd" in *More of Him, Less of Me* (Dawn Treader, LLC, 2018), 40.
2. William Shakespeare, *As You Like It*, Act 2, sc. 7, l.139-143.
3. Epictetus, *The Art of Living* (New York: HarperCollins, 1994), 24.

192

VI.

Psalm 130

A song of ascents.

Out of the depths I cry to you, O Lord;
   O Lord, hear my voice.
Let your ears be attentive
   to my cry for mercy.
If you, O Lord, kept a record of sins,
   O Lord, who could stand?
But with you there is forgiveness;
   therefore you are feared.
I wait for the Lord, my soul waits,
   and in His word I put my hope.
My soul waits for the Lord
   more than watchmen wait for the morning,
   more than watchmen wait for the morning.
O Israel, put your hope in the Lord,
   for with the Lord is unfailing love
   and with Him is full redemption.
He Himself will redeem Israel
   from all their sins.

The Fifty-ninth Hour

Psalm 130:1—Out of the depths I cry to you, O Lord....

T o be your man, O Lord,

   sometimes means the bottom
     of a dry cistern,
where the confines are dark and dank,
   the walls are tight and tall,
     and the world above reduced
   to a small shaft
     of untouchable light.
How he finds himself in the depths
   seldom matters—
for maybe it was his own doing,
     the end result of a youthful arrogance
      that had to be stripped
     of its gaudy robe.
But maybe it wasn't.
   And maybe the truth he spoke
     simply cut too close,
   and jealousy fed
     the plans of petty men.
Yet either way, Lord,
   we are told to think
   your purpose put him there—
betrayed, framed, imprisoned,
   out of the confines of a cistern,
   into the depths of a dungeon—
and still that small shaft
   of untouchable light
     on which hope hangs.
       ~

One day, Lord, your man
   may stand before his enemies to say,
   "You intended to harm me,
     but God intended it for good."
But to the man in the depths—
   the man who is not yet
     a man of retrospect—

the depths seem no less deep,
  and the promise
    of your good intentions
  often a cold comfort.
For tomorrow seems like forever,
  and today seems like eternity…
but for that small shaft
  of untouchable light
  that shoots across the darkness.
For there is a window in each day,
  when the angle is just right,
where that light falls upon the man
  kneeling in the darkness
  as he cries out to you.
And in this moment,
  small kindnesses may come:
cold skin warmed
  by the glow of a distant star,
the favor of a warden,
  and success in menial tasks—
  manna for the every day.

                ~

The light shines in the darkness,
  and the darkness cannot overcome it.
And though it seems a small,
  untouchable shaft,
when it falls upon me I am reminded:
  Neither death nor life,
    neither angels nor demons,
  neither the present nor the future,
    nor any powers,
  neither height nor depth,
    nor anything else in all creation,
  will ever separate me
    from your love, O Lord.
For one day a vision will come
  to the depths of this dungeon,
    and the cell's doors will open
  to the bright light above;
and though today's shackles
  seem no less tight,
  I will at last stand in the Light
    that makes even today seem right.

Selected Readings for Further Study

† Genesis 37:12-36

† Romans 8:28-38

Questions for Reflection and Prayer:

1. When Joseph is at the bottom of the cistern, do you think he was capable of seeing God's good intentions in the moment? Or do you think he was angry with his brothers and perhaps questioned God? How might you have responded?

2. In his exposition on Romans 8:28, Puritan preacher, Thomas Watson, says:

> God's ways are 'past finding out'(Rom. 11:33). They are rather to be admired than fathomed. There is never a providence of God, but has either a mercy or a wonder in it. How stupendous and infinite is that wisdom, that makes the most adverse dispensations work for the good of His children!

As Watson points out, part of our difficulty with difficult times is our desire to "fathom" them in the moment. What would happen if we admired them instead as part of God's infinite wisdom? Would our perspective change?

3. The Apostle Paul exhorts us to consider even difficulties within the framework of God's love (Ro 8:28). As Watson says, "Love is an expansion of the soul, or the inflaming of the affections, by which a Christian breathes after God as the supreme and sovereign good." When we love God, then all things—good and bad—work together for the good: which is of course, God Himself. Have you acknowledged God as the "supreme and sovereign good" in your life?

References
    Ge 37:12-28; 39:20-23; 50:20; Ro 8:28-38

Diving Deeper:

1. J.D. Eubanks, MD, "Set Purpose" in *More of Him, Less of Me* (Dawn Treader, LLC, 2018), 338.
2. Thomas Watson, *All Things for Good* (Gideon House Books, 2015), 53, 59.

The Sixtieth Hour

Psalm 130:2—O Lord, hear my voice.
Let your ears be attentive
to my cry for mercy.

O Lord, to love is to listen,
and to listen is to love.
Because you are Love,
  you must be listening.
But if you are anything like
  the man you made in your image,
  will your listening always be hearing?
For I confess, O Lord,
  many times I have listened,
    but haven't heard a thing.
I have seated myself
  in the presence of those I love,
    to listen without listening—
  even you have been my victim.
My body might have been there—
  at least my heart's intentions too—
  but my mind was miles away.
Like Martha, my thoughts were busy
  with more pressing things.
Did she know I was not listening?
  Could he see the inattention in my eyes?
But Mary sat at your feet listening
  to everything you had to say, Lord.
And though you knew without looking,
  she was listening to your every word—
  for you knew her inside and out—
    you could *see* the listening in her look:
  the hunger of broken eyes
    eating all you had to say.
              ~
In this hour, I confess, Lord,
  I long to see this look of listening
    on your rapturous face.

198

I dream of sitting close enough
   to see the love in your eyes
   as I pour out my heart.
But then I imagine you walking
      the endless shore
   of the human sea you have made,
watching the waves crash at your feet
   as they send up a mist of dissolution,
   with roars of frustration.
Amidst this call of countless voices
   falling upon your ears,
      how can you hear one cry
   in this chorus of considerations?
Who am I to expect
   the attention of your ear,
      when I am one of a multitude,
   and my cry will soon be covered
   in the crashing weight of another's?
But when the righteous cry out,
      the Lord hears them;
   He delivers them from all their troubles.
The Lord is close to the brokenhearted
   and saves those who are crushed in spirit.
                        ~

Mary sat listening to all you had to say, Lord,
   and in the love of her listening
   you were listening in love.
Maybe the lesson of listening
   lies in the broken raptness
   of her heart's attention—
      and that you, O Lord,
   listen to the listening spirit.
And while we are still waves upon that sea,
      full of our own rising and falling,
   we are just part of a distant roar in your ear,
      until we break alone
         on the shore before your feet.
Then, like the woman
   who has chosen what is better,
   your ear will hear us without a word,
      and your mercy will not be taken away;
   for your love has listened,
      and your listening has loved.

† Psalm 34:17-18

† Luke 10:38-42

Questions for Reflection and Prayer:

1. Both Martha and Mary loved Jesus. But they demonstrated that love in different ways. Jesus praises Mary, however, for choosing what is better. What did Mary choose? What lesson does her choice teach us?

2. Listening to someone is both one of the easiest and hardest things to do. It simultaneously requires of us both nothing and everything. As a result, why is listening a form of love?

3. Chinese gospel teacher, Watchman Nee, says the following:

> We can touch a person's spirit by *listening* to what he says. When a man is speaking, we have to pay attention not only to the things he is saying but to the condition of his spirit. We do not know men merely by their words but by their spirits.

When Jesus commends Mary, He was paying attention to the "condition" of her spirit. What is the condition of your spirit as you listen to the Lord?

References
> Ps 34:17-18; Lk 10:38-42; Jn 12:1-8

Diving Deeper:

1. J.D. Eubanks, MD, "Listening Carefully" in *More of Him, Less of Me* (Dawn Treader, LLC, 2018), 13.
2. Watchman Nee, *The Breaking of the Outer Man and the Release of the Spirit* (Anaheim, CA: Living Stream Ministry, 1997), 52.

The Sixty-first Hour

Psalm 130:3—If you, O Lord, kept a record of sins,
O Lord, who could stand?

O Lord, so much depends upon
        if—
for *if* Cain had only done what is right,
   he would have been accepted,
and the sin crouching at his door,
   mastered by the Master within.
But he didn't, as so many don't,
   and he went out from your Presence, Lord,
   into a wandering land.
If the Israelites were only careful
   to observe all your commands, Father—
to love the Lord their God,
   to walk in all His ways
   and to hold fast to Him—
then every place they set their foot
   would have been theirs forever,
      and no nation
   would have been able
      to stand against them.
But they didn't, as so many don't,
   and the Lion left His lair
   to lay the land desolate.
And *if* the wise King Solomon
   had only been wise enough
to walk before you
   with integrity of heart,
then the temple he built
   would still be standing.
But he didn't, as so many don't,
   and he gave his heart away
   to a thousand demons in dress;
and the great temple fell
   into a pile of rubble.
        ~

201

Then the old covenant
   gave way to the new,
and Love came gently down,
   unconditionally,
      if it weren't for His conditions—
for *if* you will to be forgiven,
   you must forgive;
if you long to bear fruit,
   you must remain in the vine;
if you want to show God your love,
   you must obey;
if you desire to save your life,
   you must lose it;
if you will to follow where He leads,
   you must pick up your cross;
and only *if* you believe in the Son,
   will you see eternal life—
for only *if* the Son sets you free,
   will you be free indeed:
   so much depends upon...
      if.
For no one will be dragged
   into your heavenly courts, O Lord;
and even hell is that choice
   you give with lock and key,
if a man insists on shutting the gates
   on your reckless, unrelenting love.
For no sacrifice for sins is left,
   for the one who keeps on sinning
   in the face of the Truth—
only the fearful expectation
   of the judgement he has chosen,
      and the raging fire
   he has brought upon himself.
If only
   he had chosen what is better...
for if you, O Lord, kept a record of sins,
   O Lord, who could stand?
But that is what we must not miss...*if*—
   for *if* we die with you,
      we will rise with you,
and our endless record of sins
   will be nothing but blank pages.

Selected Readings for Further Study

† Deuteronomy 11:22-28

† John 15:5-11

Questions for Reflection and Prayer:

1. In both the Old Testament and the New, God's communication with man often uses the conditional word "*if*." Of course, if God is omnipotent, then nothing would need to be conditional. He could simply make it happen. So why has God set up a world where the way to Him is so full of "ifs"? Does this reality make God less or more spectacular?

2. During his discussion of hell, C.S. Lewis says, "I willingly believe that the damned are, in one sense, successful, rebels to the end; that the doors of hell are locked on the *inside*." As Lewis stresses, the agency for separation from God lies with these spiritual rebels—the lock is on the inside, not the outside. Interestingly, God made this nightmare possible. Why would a loving God allow that?

3. Jesus says, "I tell you the truth, everyone who sins is a slave to sin. Now a slave has no permanent place in the family, but a son belongs to it forever. So if the Son sets you free, you will be free indeed" (Jn 8:34-36). Lewis goes on to say, "They [the damned] enjoy forever the horrible freedom they have demanded, and are therefore self-enslaved: just as the blessed, forever submitting to obedience, become through all eternity more and more free." God's world of "ifs" is a choice for freedom. What kind of freedom have you chosen?

References
Ge 4:7; Dt 11:22-28; 1 Ki 9:1-9; Isa 7:9; Jer 15:19; 25:7-38; Mt 6:14-15; 16:24-25; 17:20; 21:22; Lk 4:7; Jn 8:36; 15:5-11; Ro 5:10, 15; 6:8; 1 Cor 16:22; Heb 10:26-27

Diving Deeper:

1. J.D. Eubanks, MD, "Choices" in *More of Him, Less of Me* (Dawn Treader, LLC, 2018), 102.
2. C.S. Lewis, *The Problem of Pain* (New York: HarperOne, 1996), 130.

Psalm 130:4—But with you [Lord] there is forgiveness;
therefore you are feared.

I fear you, O Lord,

not merely for your power
to throw the body and soul
  into the eternal fire,
but more for your strength
    to forgive
  the unforgiveable in me.
For forgiveness is a violent gentleness,
  full of a two-edged suffering—
a sword that pierces the heart,
  and then twists the blade
  to make sure its steel is felt,
before returning bloodied to its scabbard
  to let the wounded heal.
And for that bleeding man
  to forgive just one trespass,
    may bring him
  to the brink of death.
But to forgive them all,
  and to go on forgiving them,
that is an unfathomable torture—
  a work of love beyond understanding.
When I consider the agony,
  I tremble before the affection
that knowingly gave man
  the freedom to inflict this pain.
I quiver before the Love
  that might have spared Himself misery,
    but chose a long suffering instead.
For love always risks a broken heart,
  and even you, God,
    are no exception to your rule.
So your wrath, Lord, is to be feared,
  but nothing compared to your love.

For it is a power beyond comprehension—
    an ocean with no bounds or borders,
    no bottom to touch our toes.
When your love swallows a man,
    it swallows him whole;
and only when he is coughed up,
    transformed on some distant shore,
does he find he's no longer just a man,
    but a mission minted by Love.
I am held as in a vise,
    constrained by this love of God.[15]
Yet to my shame, some part of me
        still resists the hold,
    for there is an inner rebel on the run,
and an addict still high
    on the lingering ecstasy of self.
For to be forgiven by you, Lord,
    means accepting I am nothing
    and you are everything;
it means I can't, but you can;
    it means forgiveness
    is the cross I now must bear.
So forgiveness is a fearful thing,
    and the God who forgives
        the unforgiveable in me,
    is a God to be feared above all things.
Yet who is the servant who leaves this Master
        forgiven of the unforgiveable,
    only to demand pennies from the paupers
        who ask forgiveness of him?
Is it not the little man left in me,
    whose debt you paid
        to set him free?
O Lord, in this hour I pray,
    help me to always see,
that though I am debt free,
    the debt of love I owe to thee
        is a fortune with a constant calling.

---

[15] Oswald Chambers, *My Utmost for His Highest* (Grand Rapids, MI: Discovery House Publishers, 2012), November 20.

† Jonah 1:17-2:10

† Matthew 18:21-35

Questions for Reflection and Prayer:

1. As Henri Nouwen points out, many of us struggle with the idea of God's forgiveness of our sins. He says, "One of the greatest challenges of the spiritual life is to receive God's forgiveness. There is something in us...that keeps us clinging to our sins and prevents us from letting God erase our past and offer us a completely new beginning." Why can forgiveness be so hard to receive?

2. C.S. Lewis notes that forgiving a single injury against us is hard enough. But the Christian is called to something else entirely: "...to forgive the incessant provocations of daily life—to keep on forgiving the bossy mother-in-law, the bullying husband, the nagging wife, the selfish daughter, the deceitful son—how can we do it?" Indeed, how can God do it for us?

3. The Parable of the Unmerciful Servant reminds Christians to never forget the debt they have been forgiven by the Master. The cancellation of the debt of sin results in a debt of love with ongoing commitments to both the Master and His other servants. For as Kierkegaard says, "when a man is gripped by love, he feels that this is like being in infinite debt." When was the last time you carefully considered your infinite debt of love?

References
        Jonah 1:17-2:10; Mt 10:28; 18:21-35; Eph 3:18-19

Diving Deeper:

1. J.D. Eubanks, MD, "The First Step Starts With You" in *More of Him, Less of Me* (Dawn Treader, LLC, 2018), 304.
2. Henri Nouwen, *The Return of the Prodigal Son* (New York: Image Books, 1994), 53.
3. C.S. Lewis, *The Weight of Glory* (New York: HarperOne, 2001), 182.
4. Søren Kierkegaard, *Works of Love* (New York: HarperPerennial, 2009), 172.

The Sixty-third Hour

Psalm 130:5-6—I wait for the Lord, my soul waits,
and in His word I put my hope.
My soul waits for the Lord
more than watchmen wait for the morning,
more than watchmen wait for the morning.

O Lord, this is the night
before your dawn,
and the darkness before your light.
Many lie in the comfort of warm beds
and reassuring arms,
while you have placed me here
in the path of parapets,
to traverse a bodiless, black sea
filled with some monstrous truths.
For I am the King's man,
duty-bound to confront the night
and all the demons she hides.
I know the morning will come,
and I watch for the slightest glow
with eager expectation.
But my eyes fail, looking for your promise, God;
I say, "When will you comfort me?"
For in these midnight hours,
I confess, O Lord,
the night seems interminable,
hope a pitiable evil among evils,
and the coming dawn far less real
than the wraiths of these black hours.
Almighty Counselor and King,
where would I be without your Word,
for it is the lamp to my feet
and the light for my path!
Still, in the watches of this long night,
I confess, Lord, I recite your promises
as much to convince myself they're real,
as to comfort my weary heart
and steady my tired feet.

207

For in the darkness,
    sometimes it all seems the same—
        guessing, groping,
    with or without great promises,
        we all still stumble along.
And if it were not for your light, Lord,
    then every step
        would be without true direction;
    every lonesome path,
        just a lonesome path.
But with you, Lord, there is light in the night;
    though the end is still unseen,
    the next step I can know.
For even if I say,
    *"Surely the darkness will hide me
        and the light become night around me,"
    even the darkness will not be dark to you;
        the night will shine like the day,
        for darkness is as light to you.*
And when this Light nestles
    in the heart of a man,
then the Word becomes flesh again,
    and beats into perfect rhythm
        the anxious organ
    striding the parapets of the night.
The morning's promises
    become midnight's certainties,
as the One whom I once felt as far,
    stoops to the sacred
        nearness of knowing.
For the man of the moment,
    hope may be a fool's errand,
an evil better kept in her box,
    than unleashed on a world
        of would-be saints.
But for the man of mission,
    no moment is without meaning;
and whether he is swimming
    in the sun's gentle surf,
or walking amidst the balustrades
    of the darkest hours,
he hopes in the inerrant Word,
    as he waits in certain hope.

Selected Readings for Further Study

† Jeremiah 31:31-34

† Titus 2:11-14

Questions for Reflection and Prayer:

1. As the Apostle John tells us, Christ is the Word (Jn 1:1). If we love Christ, we will love the Word. For as A.W. Tozer says, "...if my love for the Scriptures has cooled even a little, if my eagerness to eat and drink the inspired Word has abated by as much as one degree, I should humbly admit that I have missed God's signal somewhere and frankly backtrack until I find the true way once more." When you feel lost in the darkness, do you backtrack to the Word to find your way again?

2. The young Albert Camus once said, "For the body knows nothing of hope. All it knows is the beating of its own heart." While Camus' statement may have some biologic truth, it spiritually misses the mark. For when Christ enters the Christian's heart, the body and soul are aware of the heartbeat of Christ. And as Christ is hope (1 Tim 1:1; Tit 2:13), the body housing the living Christ can do nothing but hope, even on days when hope is difficult. Is your heart beating with the hope of Christ?

3. In Greek mythology, Pandora was the first created woman who was given by the gods a box filled with "beautiful" evils. Hope was in that box of evils. But when Pandora's curiosity caused her to open the lid, the evils escaped—except for hope. A world where hope never leaves the box is a bleak world. But the Apostle Paul reminds us of our "blessed hope"(Tit 2:13)—Christ—and the glorious appearing yet to come. Is your hope inside the box or in Christ and His return?

References
　　　Ex 34:6-7; Dt 22:8; Ps 119:74, 81-88, 105; 139:11-12; Jer 31:31-34;
　　　Jn 1:4-5, 14; Tim 1:1; Tit 2:13

Diving Deeper:

1. J.D. Eubanks, MD, "Befriending Darkness" in *More of Him, Less of Me* (Dawn Treader, LLC, 2018), 326.
2. Albert Camus, "The Desert" in *Personal Writings* (New York: Vintage International, 2020), 101.
3. A.W. Tozer, *Man, The Dwelling Place of God* (Public Domain)

🐌

The Sixty-fourth Hour

Psalm 130:7-8—O Israel, put your hope in the Lord,
for with the Lord is unfailing love
and with Him is full redemption.
He Himself will redeem Israel
from all their sins.

Forgiveness from the heart, Lord,

is a frightful endeavor,
for it never comes in half-measures;
and to forgive as you have forgiven me,
means my heart—like yours—must go out
into the storm of suffering.
Who knows if redemption will follow,
for it is a costly commodity,
whose currency is always blood,
and whose coffer always love.
And who but you, Lord,
has a strongbox large enough
to forgive the sin in me,
much less the many "Me" in multiple?
Sooner or later, a man will bleed to death,
and his stores of love
are not limitless vaults.
But then you tell me there is no end
to the richness of your affection,
for it is a treasure chest without bottom,
an unfailing reserve
you invite me to swim in.
Shall I take the plunge
into this rolling sea of gold?
For you say I shall arise into wealth,
fists full of more coin
than any debt I'll ever owe.
It is a beautiful tale full of wizardry,
fit for leprechauns and fairies,
but for the blood
by which the story is written.

For blood is the only truth
  that never lies,
and to have written your lines
    in a crimson tide,
  means redemption must be real.
You have been saying it all along:
  Before the Nile turned red
    at the feet of Pharaoh—
    "I will redeem you
    with an outstretched arm";
  to a people clothed in offenses,
    prostrate before sacred stones—
    "Return to me,
    for I have redeemed you";
  and to the wayward hearts
    living the lie we often live—
    "I long to redeem them...."
You are my Redeemer, Lord,
  the Mighty One of Jacob,
and the lyrics of love
  you have been singing
    since the beginning,
  are the redemption song
    my heart hangs on.
No greater love exists than this—
  a man chooses to lay down his life
    for the sake of another.
And you, Lord, laid it down
  of your own accord,
    the blood of One
  for the blood of many.
This is the mystery of your will:
    Redemption—
  in, through, only by you:
the one thing I can never do,
  no matter how tall my tower.
For the obelisk of man
  shall never pierce Heaven,
but the nails through your body
  parted both the curtain and the clouds,
to do what only Love can do—
  redeem the irredeemable in me.

211

† Genesis 11:1-9

† Ephesians 1:3-14

Questions for Reflection and Prayer:

1. Redemption is the essence of God's metanarrative. What does redemption mean? How are we redeemed? And, more fundamentally, why does redemption matter (Ro 3:21-26)?

2. Whether in the Old Testament or the New, there is no redemption without blood (Heb 9:22). Why do you think God designed a plan of atonement dependent upon blood? Why would He orchestrate a story in which He Himself would have to bleed to bring that story to completion? What is the point of the blood?

3. In contemplating Christianity, Kierkegaard asks, "Why must he [a man] be a Christian when it is so hard?" In answer to his question, he provides an absolute and a relative response. Concerning the latter he says, "Because the consciousness of sin within him [the man] will not leave him in peace, the pain of it fortifies him to bear everything else, if only he can find *redemption*."

As Kierkegaard reminds us, Christianity is nothing but "lunacy" unless it provides the *redemption* our hearts long for. Why do you think our hearts long for *redemption*? How does Kierkegaard's perspective fit into God's metanarrative?

References
> Ge 11:1-9; Ex 6:6; Isa 43:1; 44:22; 47:4; 49:26; 62:12; Zec 10:8; Hos 7:13; 13:14; Jn 10:17-18; Ro 3:24; Eph 1:7; Col 1:14; Heb 9:12

Diving Deeper:

1. J.D. Eubanks, MD, "Forgiveness From the Heart" in *More of Him, Less of Me* (Dawn Treader, LLC, 2018), 116.
2. Søren Kierkegaard, *The Diary of Søren Kierkegaard* (New York: Citadel Press, 1988), 149-150.

VII.

Psalm 143

A psalm of David

O Lord, hear my prayer,
  listen to my cry for mercy;
in your faithfulness and righteousness
  come to my relief.
Do not bring your servant into judgement,
  for no one living is righteous before you.
The enemy pursues me,
  he crushes me to the ground;
he makes me dwell in darkness
  like those long dead.
So my spirit grows faint within me;
  my heart within me is dismayed.
I remember the days of long ago;
  I meditate on all your works
  and consider what your hands have done.
I spread out my hands to you;
  my soul thirsts for you like a parched land.
Answer me quickly, O Lord;
  my spirit fails.
Do not hide your face from me
  or I will be like those who go down to the pit.
Let the morning bring me word
  of your unfailing love,
  for I have put my trust in you.
Show me the way I should go,
  for to you I lift up my soul.

Rescue me from my enemies, O Lord,
  for I hide myself in you.
Teach me to do your will,
  for you are my God;
may your good Spirit
  lead me on level ground.
For your name's sake, O Lord, preserve my life;
  in your righteousness, bring me out of trouble.
In your unfailing love, silence my enemies;
  destroy all my foes,
    for I am your servant.

The Sixty-fifth Hour

Psalm 143:1—O Lord, hear my prayer,
listen to my cry for mercy;
in your faithfulness and righteousness
come to my relief.

Mercy is the muscle

you use, O Lord,
to move the hearts of men—
the rough hands that work
the soil of souls,
until the baked ground yields
to give the seed somewhere to grow.
Only idols have beautiful hands,
with long, elegant fingers
stretched out in eternal repose.
They are beautiful, but bootless,
and the ineffable grace they promise
remains set in the stillness of stone.
But God's hands belong to the fields—
they are weathered by the sun,
and thickened by the work of crushing
so many rock-ribbed
hearts in hiding.
Forgiveness is full of this violence,
and the heart that seeks life
must break forth from the stone—
for there is no other way.
But so few can see it—
mercy moving in the dismantling of man:
in the shattering of the outer shell,
so the inner life might break through
with the Kingdom's brilliance.
For even the seasoned saint may struggle
to perceive purpose
in your hammering compassion, Lord;
and the sledge that keeps coming
to crush the monolith of man,
seems a brutal kindness.

215

Why break the monuments you've made?
  Why crush the hearts you've formed?
Shouldn't mercy be just
  a soft pillow to fall upon,
    and compassion,
  nothing but a welcoming embrace?
But then, for a moment, I dare to be you, God,
  and I know I would never choose
    to hug a stone,
  if I might have flesh instead.
Knowing this, who knows why
  you hid tender hearts in outer shells;
why the hammer of your Spirit's rough hands
    must break to bits
  the man you have made?
But maybe the magic of mercy
  lies embedded in the ignoble rock
  between man and his Maker.
And maybe the gifts of compassion
    and forgiveness—
  that bring God to man
    and man to men—
cannot break into the world
  without the breaking of man.
Till you smash the stone,
  a deadly distance remains;
and only your violent gentleness
  removes the surrounding rock
  to free the diamond within.
But even then, without those facets,
  there is little brilliance or fire.
For only the continued chiseling
  of your baffling mercy, Lord,
    creates a glittering jewel
    capable of capturing
      the Glory of Heaven.
O Lord, hear my prayer,
  listen to my cry for mercy;
in your faithfulness and righteousness,
  come to my relief.
May the muscle of your mercy
    cleave my stone,
  till this heart of flesh cleaves only to you.

Selected Readings for Further Study

† Micah 7:14-20

† John 12:23-28

Questions for Reflection and Prayer:

1. To become the recipient of mercy, we must be in the hands of one who has power over us. Compassion and forgiveness go hand-in-hand with this mercy. Most often, we want to view mercy as an unrelenting "kindness." But have you considered that forgiveness and compassion might—and often do—also take the form of God's disciplining work in your life? Is there still kindness in this form of mercy?

2. Chinese gospel preacher, Watchman Nee, believes a spiritual life is impossible unless God breaks the "outer man." He says, "The Holy Spirit has only one goal in all His disciplining work: To break and dismantle the outer man so that the inner man can break forth." Has the Spirit broken your "outer man"?

3. Japanese theologian, Kosuke Koyama, says, "Merciful hands must show themselves as hard, worn hands, not as beautiful attractive hands….The Holy Spirit has something to do, then, with the wrinkled faces and rough hands." The Lord is a "merciful God" who is "always at His work"(Dt 4:31; Jn 5:17). His hands are worker's hands; and those rough hands are full of mercy. Does your spiritual life have the wrinkled face and rough hands of God's mercy?

References
> Ex 33:19; Dt 4:31; Joel 2:12-14; Mic 7:18-19; Jn 5:17-18; 12:23-28;
> Ro 7:22; 2 Cor 2:11-18; 4:16; Eph 3:16

Diving Deeper:

1. J.D. Eubanks, MD, "Always Working" in *More of Him, Less of Me* (Dawn Treader, LLC, 2018), 31.
2. Watchman Nee, *The Breaking of the Outer Man and the Release of the Spirit* (Anaheim, CA: Living Stream Ministry, 1997), 10.
3. Kosuke Koyama, *The Three Mile an Hour God* (London: SCM Press, 2021), 50.

The Sixty-sixth Hour

Psalm 143:2—Do not bring your [the Lord's] servant into judgement,
for no one living is righteous before you.

O Lord, this world is full of traps:
  hooks, lines, and snares,
    thrown out across a dark forest floor.
Every step might be a fatal one,
  where the trap's teeth dive deep
    into the softness of blind feet.
But even when the hooks don't set
  and the snares don't catch,
    how we might struggle
  to free ourselves in this fight for life!
Who is the hunter of my heart—
    the brain behind
  these many booby-traps?
Is he in the dark out there,
  or might he have one foot
    in the midnight of me too?
Am I a victim of his schemes,
  or a knowing accomplice
    too well-informed to see well?
Error seldom comes dressed
  in black and white,
    and the deadliest traps
  live in the liminal light.
Sometimes the best seeing comes
  when I question all I see;
and the man who is most at risk,
  is the one whose vision
    has never dared
  the double-take of doubt.
Folly often falls
  into one of two securities:
the confidence that sees no demons
  and denies Divinity's sovereignty;
and the reckless righteousness of rightness,
  with its flowing robes of infallibility—

218

Two diverging trails
       paved in the Liar's pitches
   and signposted with his promises.
But both roads lead to the same death,
   and the judgement will not fail
   to fall upon their false gods.
For no one stands righteous before you, Lord;
   the flamboyant sinner
     and the self-styled saint,
   are simply two iterations of the same.
All men are hypocrites,
   but the only men beyond hope
     are those who fail to see
   their own hypocrisy.
That is our enemy's subtle play—
   the seeing that is not seeing,
     and the vision that spots a speck,
   but fails to espy the plank.
In this hour I confess, O Lord,
   to the Pharisee in me,
and to all those devotions I have given
   towards a religion which is not yours.
For I have been careful to give
   a tenth of my spices.
But has my duty neglected
   justice, mercy, and faithfulness?
Have I strained out a gnat,
   only to swallow a camel?
Does my clean cup mean I clean,
   or am I nothing
   but a whitewashed tomb?
O Lord, do not bring your servant
     into judgement,
   for my brood of vipers
     will not escape your fire.
But look instead upon your Son,
   and in the fondness of your affection,
remember the heel
   that crushed the serpent's head.
For beneath those pierced feet,
   high and lifted up,
   I am righteous in your eyes.

219

† Proverbs 3:21-26

† Matthew 23

Questions for Reflection and Prayer:

1. A.W. Tozer says, "The whole world has been booby-trapped by the devil, and the deadliest trap of all is the religious one. Error never looks so innocent as when it is found in the sanctuary." As Tozer reminds us, religious security—whether in the church and its members or in our dutiful devotions—can lead to the worst kind of error. Jesus repeatedly denounced the Pharisees for this kind of error.

When was the last time you considered your own hypocrisy? Have you recognized your inner Pharisee and asked for the Spirit's grace to keep rooting him out? Instead of finding your security in yourself or your own righteousness, where does God want you to find your security instead (Pr 18:10)?

2. The twin traps of self-empowered godlessness and religious hypocrisy both ensnare through a twisted confidence. Ironically, however, confidence is the best way to avoid the world's traps. But where does this confidence come from? Solomon says, "for the Lord will be your confidence, and will keep your foot from being snared"(Pr 3:26). Have you placed your confidence in the Lord?

3. In his poem, "In Memoriam A.H.H.," Alfred, Lord Tennyson says, "There lives more faith in honest doubt,/ Believe me, than in half the creeds." In the life of faith, should we fear doubt or the confidence that never doubts? Which is potentially more dangerous?

References
Ge 3:8-15; Pr 3:21-26; 18:10; Mt 7:1-6; 23

Diving Deeper:

1. J.D. Eubanks, MD, "Stumbling Blocks" in *More of Him, Less of Me* (Dawn Treader, LLC, 2018), 276.
2. A.W. Tozer, *Man, The Dwelling Place of God* (Public Domain).
3. Alfred, Lord Tennyson, "In Memoriam A.H.H." (Public Domain).

The Sixty-seventh Hour

Psalm 143:3—The enemy pursues me,
he crushes me to the ground;
he makes me dwell in darkness
like those long dead.

Lord of light,

there is no darkness
like the darkness of the soul;
for it is an inner night,
black as pitch
painted on the windows
of a weary heart
and an addled mind.
When a man gets lost inside,
it seems pointless to tell him
there is still a world
of beauty and light.
For the darkness he finds himself in
may swallow
even the walls defining his confinement,
as the voices of those long dead
try to drown out God's rescuing call—
deaf to it all—
unless, with a sigh you say, "*Ephphatha!*"[16]
For until you, Lord, break in
and pull him out, every direction
seems only a blind grasp at air.
Seldom is a man dragged against his will
down one of the many roads leading
from the light into this night.
And more often than not,
he is slowly coaxed
by some version of himself—
a demon dressed in mirror's image—
wielding a twisted reasoning
that sells itself to the self,
on the pretense of perfect sense.

---

[16] "be opened"

221

For the devil knows too well
　　to come as the devil,
and the enemy a man least suspects,
　　is the man within
　　　the man himself.
Such is Satan's sleight of hand,
　　that knowing himself powerless
　　to conquer the man without the man,
simply makes himself into the man,
　　　who can talk himself into drinking
　　the cup he would never have drunk.
Yet when he has gulped it down,
　　what does the sinner taste on his tongue,
　　　but despair?
For no matter what the devil offers,
　　he gives no other wine.
Still, even the bitterness of this drink
　　might hook the unmoored mind,
if only the darkness divorces
　　the truth of the light from his life.
And what once looked black, now is white;
　　what once tasted bitter, now tastes sweet;
　　and what once was evil, now seems good.
For isn't the unrepentant wise in his own eyes
　　and clever in his own sight?
He might even revel in his despair,
　　and pleasure in the consciousness
　　　of his pitiful position.
So only you, Lord, can pull a man
　　from the clutches of his nightmare…
if only his troubled slumber
　　　reaches for the rescue
　　that calls him back to the day.
But when he rises out of the pit,
　　sobered up from his drunken night,
　　　it remains for the penitent
　　to fight the good fight,
with his battered heart shielded
　　in the breastplate of faith and love,
and his wandering mind covered
　　in the helmet of salvation's hope.
For there in the darkness I chose the light;
　　and now, O Lord, I fight your fight.

Selected Readings for Further Study

† Isaiah 5:20-21

† 1 Thessalonians 5:4-11

Questions for Reflection and Prayer:

1. Every life knows dark times and moments of despair. But Christians do not remain there. For as the Apostle Paul reminds the Thessalonians, "You are all sons of the light and sons of the day. We do not belong to the night or to the darkness"(1 Thes 5:5). Does your heart *belong* to the day or to the night?

2. Puritan preacher, Thomas Brooks, speaks of our culpability in sin when he says:

> That though Satan has his devices to draw souls to sin, yet we must be careful that we do not lay all our temptations upon Satan…and father that upon him that is to be fathered upon our own base hearts. I think that oftentimes men charge that upon the devil that which is to be charged upon their own hearts.

It is dangerous to deny the devil's schemes, but equally dangerous to ignore personal responsibility. Have you recognized the two-part play of sin in your life?

3. In his fictional polemic against Scottish Calvinism—*The Private Memoirs and Confessions of a Justified Sinner*—author James Hogg portrays a "justified sinner" tempted by the devil who comes in the man's own likeness. As Hogg astutely recognizes, the enemy sometimes masquerades as me. Have you paused to consider that Satan's attack against you might come to you as you?

References
    Isa 5:20-21; Mk 7:31-37; 1 Thes 5:4-11; 1 Tim 6:12

Diving Deeper:

1. J.D. Eubanks, MD, "Lovers of Light" in *More of Him, Less of Me* (Dawn Treader, LLC, 2018), 289.
2. Thomas Brooks, *Precious Remedies Against Satan's Devices* (Public Domain).
3. James Hogg, *The Private Memoirs and Confessions of a Justified Sinner* (London: Wordsworth Classics, 2003).

The Sixty-eighth Hour

Psalm 143:4—So my spirit grows faint within me;
my heart within me is dismayed.

The business of Heaven, O Lord,
  must be unmanning the man
    to make the man.
For how else do we explain
  the seismic troubles you use,
  to rattle our towers
    and crumble our walls?
Even the stoutest heart cannot escape,
  and sooner or later,
our inner castles come down,
  as the heart's hearting loosens,
  and the balustrades fall
    on iron gates ajar
  for the King's coming.
O Lord, you know best,
  the heart of the man is the man;
and when the heart is disheartened,
  the man might be reached.
For nothing shuts Heaven from hearts,
  like the absence of trouble.
So your love allows
    difficulty and disorder to disrupt
  the heart's fragile treaties of peace.
For nothing keeps us from true Peace,
    like all those place-holding pacifiers
  the soul keeps clinging to.
But Heaven's peace pierces to the heart
  by way of your sword, Lord;
and joy's contentment cannot come
    without tribulation and trials—
  for, "In this world you will have trouble."
Yet, the conundrum lies in the command:
  "Do not let your hearts be troubled,"
    when in truth, all there is
      is trouble.

224

And if it remains for reason
    to reach through this tangled mess
  for a God who lives somewhere out there,
then earth would never meet sky
    in the minds of thinking men.
For who can calculate
    divine affection, O Lord,
  from the sum of troubled things?
Who can watch an infant die
  and arrive at a knowledge of God?
And what man—except you, Lord?—
    could find himself betrayed
  by one who calls himself a friend,
    and still add it all up
  to a God who is good?
But God is grasped by the heart,
  and the heart has a mind of its own,
    with a reasoning
  reason does not recognize.
For no man can be argued
  into shouldering his cross after you, Lord;
but the logic of love
  might bear all burdens
  to set the heart ablaze.
So even when my heart, Lord,
  is distressed and dismayed,
even then, its logic might conclude,
  your love can make all things new,
as the Infinite breaks through
  the borders of my finitude
  to impart faith to the forlorn—
    if only…
Heaven inclines my heart to you.
For the heart of a man
  has a cold soul,
  unless you, my Lord, ignite its fire.
But then, with a spark,
  it might become all flame,
fanned by the bellows of Heaven
    into the eternal fire,
  that consumes the man
  to make a new man in you.

Selected Readings for Further Study

† Isaiah 48:17-22

† Matthew 10:34-39

Questions for Reflection and Prayer:

1. C.S. Lewis says, "But in this world everything is upside down. That which, if it could be prolonged here, would be truancy, is likest that which in a better country is the End of ends. Joy is the serious business of heaven." Because our world is "upside down," the business of Heaven must first be to *unman the man to make the man* before joy becomes the "End of ends." Have you had your unmanning moment before God? Have you been caught up in Heaven's business?

2. When we read the word "heart" in biblical literature, theologian Kenneth Bailey reminds us of the importance of seeing this word through the eyes of the ancient world. He says, "Modern Western culture limits the word *heart* to the feelings. But the heart in the Hebrew mind included the entire interior life of a person. The feelings, the mind and the will were all part of 'the heart.'" When God searches the heart, he searches the *whole person* (Jer 17:10). What does God see when he searches your "heart"?

3. Pascal famously says, "The heart has its reasons, which reason does not know....It is the heart which experiences God, and not the reason. " No one will come to God by reason alone. For as Pascal observes, the heart experiences God. But the heart's pull toward God is not without reason. What "reason(s)" does your heart give for loving God?

References
      Pr 4:23; 14:10, 30; 16:21; 20:5; 24:32; 28:14; Isa 48:17-22; Mt 3:11-12;
      10:34-39; Jn 14:27; 16:33; Acts 2:3-4

Diving Deeper:

1. J.D. Eubanks, MD, "Fan the Fire" in *More of Him, Less of Me* (Dawn Treader, LLC, 2018), 394.
2. C.S. Lewis, *The Business of Heaven* (New York: HarperCollins, 1984), 5.
2. Kenneth E. Bailey, *Jesus Through Middle Eastern Eyes* (Downers Grove, IL: InterVarsity Press, 2008), 84.
3. Blaise Pascal, *Pensées* (New York: Random House, 1941), 95.

226

The Sixty-ninth Hour

Psalm 143:5—I remember the days of long ago;
I meditate on all your [the Lord's] works
and consider what your hands have done.

O Lord, remembering is roulette,
for its backward reach may bring
a different fortune at every turn.
There is much I don't want to remember,
and still so much I do;
there are past days still bleeding,
even though the bloodied man
should long be dead;
and still others, brief hours,
as distant as the night's faintest stars,
that shine into the dark immensity
with their irrepressible light,
to declare something still burns brightly
in Recollection's out there.
Memory is a gift and a curse,
a hand that holds
and a dagger that plunges.
For it is one thing to live
through the moment,
in its primal pleasure or pain,
but quite another to live it again,
and then again, and again—
each time a story
with a slightly different twist—
who knows if they can be trusted?—
and a meaning that constantly morphs
as the memory slowly fades
in the face of present tensions.
But Lord, you are memory's Master too,
and when you tell us
to remember the past,
memory serves as your tool
to unearth the meaning of your movements
in past, present, and future things.

227

So when I remember the days of long ago,
* I meditate on all your works,*
* and consider what your hands have done.*
The bread you told me to keep
  and the stones you had me pile,
lead me back to distant places,
  where my lips still feel parched
  and my stomach still growls—
    even after all these years.
And I see the setting sun darkened
  by the flapping of countless wings
    falling from Heaven's floor,
and the desert's sand frosted
  in the edible flakes of your forbearance.
I watch as your staff strikes the rock,
  and water pours forth
    to satiate my quarrelsome soul.
And I pass the stones stills standing
  in the midst of Jordan's raging,
to recall the water walling up at Adam,
  to give me dry, safe passage
    into your land of promise.
These things I remember
* as I pour out my soul:*
how I used to go with the multitude,
* leading the procession to the house of God,*
with shouts of joy and thanksgiving
* among the festive throng.*
So that even now, in this downcast hour,
  my heart hopes
  in the remembrance of you, Lord,
    for you are the lifter of my head.
And though memory of former things
  pulls at my heart's scabs,
each wound testifies
  to some small triumph
  in your reclamation of this rebel.
For in remembering, I am reminded:
  You are God, and there is no other;
*   you are the Lord, and there is none like you;*
* what you have said, that will you bring about;*
*   what you have planned, that will you do.*
Lord, I remember to remember you!

† Exodus 16

† Ephesians 2:13-19

Questions for Reflection and Prayer:

1. We live in a "cancel culture" that is attempting to systematically erase history. Yet, no matter how painful our history may be, is erasure the right answer? Theologian Nicholas Wolterstorff says, "*Remembering*: one of the profoundest features of the Christian and Jewish way of being-in-the-world and being-in-history is remembering….We are to hold the past in remembrance and not let it slide away. For in history we find God." Do we become stronger by forgetting or remembering? What does God say (Isa 46: 8-9)?

2. As he reflects on his own country's conduct leading up to the bombing of Hiroshima, Japanese theologian Kosuke Koyama says, "we must take history seriously to the extent that we realize our own blindness. Those who attempt to forget history will likely repeat the mistakes of history because they do not realize their own 'blindness.'" Are you taking your life history seriously?

3. In his lecture for the 1986 Nobel Peace Prize, author Elie Wiesel says, "Without memory, our existence would be barren and opaque, like a prison cell into which no light penetrates; like a tomb which rejects the living…it is memory that will save humanity." While Wiesel's conclusion on the ultimate agency of salvation misses the mark, his point on the salvific quality of memory in our lives is—as Dostoevsky and others have also pointed out—spot on. How has God used memory in your life to "save" you?

References
    Ex 16; 17:1-7; Jos 3; 4:19-24; Ps 3:3; 42:4-6; Isa 46:8-14; Eph 2:13-19

Diving Deeper:

1. J.D. Eubanks, MD, "Remembering Our Way Out of the Pit" in *More of Him, Less of Me* (Dawn Treader, LLC, 2018), 49.
2. Nicholas Wolterstorff, *Lament for a Son* (Grand Rapids, MI: WM.B. Eerdmans, 1987), 28.
3. Kosuke Koyama, *Three Mile an Hour God* (London: SCM Press, 2021), 116.
4. https://www.nobelprize.org/prizes/peace/1986/wiesel/lecture/ (accessed 3/10/2023)

Psalm 143:6—I spread out my hands to you [God];
my soul thirsts for you like a parched land.

Holy, holy, holy,
holy are the hands that hold me!
Your hands alone, O Lord,
are holy enough
to hold hands with Heaven.
And yet, because you are holy,
you demand unholy hands holy:
high and lifted up,
palms full of a beating heart—
Does it beat for you?
You will hide your eyes
until sanguineous palms come clean.
But can a man cut out his heart
and give it to you
without blood on his hands?
Can he sacrifice his soul
on the altar of his old artifice
without a pool of red?
For there is no way to you, O Lord,
that is not paved in crimson;
and I cannot come to where you are,
unless my outstretched hands
have bled alongside yours.
Some counselors tell me:
if I devote my heart to you,
and stretch out my arms to you,
if I put away the sin that is in my hands
and allow no evil to dwell in my tent,
then I will lift up my face without shame,
and stand firm without fear.
But won't my hands still be bloody,
and won't by guilt still remain?
And if I'm fearless in the face of Holiness,
then I must be as righteous
as the Righteous One Himself.

But no man comes to your throne, God,
  dressed in the robes he has made;
and no matter what laws he keeps,
  he will never wash himself
  in the whiteness of heavenly places.
For the color of the King's cotton only comes
  through the bloody paradox:
    by the Blood, the bloodied are cleansed.
It is an argument beyond reason;
    and yet in your patience, Lord,
  you deign to reason with unreasonable men.
From the great court you say,
  "Though your sins are like scarlet,
    they shall be white as snow;
    though they are as red as crimson,
    they shall be like wool."
But many men make a mockery
  of your loving logic, O Lord,
and insist instead, on bloodying their hands
    over the washboards
    of deluded consciences,
as their frenzied efforts for white
  only stain their garments with bloody hands.
And though the outstretched arms
  of their fervent prayers
    protest a reach for Heaven's holiness,
what they give to you
  is not a beating heart in hand,
but an open palm full of warning,
  from a life already in departure.
O Lord, you know the called
  before they even come calling;
and when you set eternity
  in the hearts of men,
you knew your call of love
  would meet the defiance
    of many bloody hands.
But my heart, O Lord, is in my hands,
  and my heart cries out to you,
  "Seek His face!"
  Your face, Lord, I will seek."
May the bloody logic of Heaven, Lord,
  make this bloody man clean.

231

Selected Readings for Further Study

† Job 11:1-20

† 1 Timothy 2:1-8

Questions for Reflection and Prayer:

1. When Isaiah sees God, the budding prophet hears the angels calling out, "Holy, holy, holy is the Lord Almighty; the whole earth is full of His glory"(Isa 6:3). At the sight of this holiness, Isaiah is quick to recognize his "unclean lips." What does God do to bridge the gap between Holy and unholy? Has a coal of God's fire touched you?

2. Poet Rainer Rilke recognizes the tension of the divine call. He says:

> For my call is always filled with departure; against such a powerful
> current you cannot move. Like an outstretched arm
> is my call. And its hand, held open and reaching up
> to seize, remains in front of you, open
> as if in defense and warning,
> Ungraspable One, far above.

Are you called, but not coming? Is your hand open to grasp the hand of Heaven, or is it an outstretched STOP sign against the divine reach?

3. What does Solomon mean when he says God has set eternity in the heart (Ecc 3:11)? Can you feel the call of eternity in your heart?

References
Lev 20:26; 1 Ki 8:54; Neh 8:6; Job 11:13-20; Ps 63:4; 88:9; 134:2; 141:2; Ecc 3:11; Isa 1:15-18; 6:1-7; La 3:41; 1 Tim 2:8

Diving Deeper:

1. J.D. Eubanks, MD, "Because" in *More of Him, Less of Me* (Dawn Treader, LLC, 2018), 241.
2. Rainer Maria Rilke, "Seventh Elegy" in *Duino Elegies & The Sonnets to Orpheus* (New York: Vintage International, 2009), 47.

The Seventy-first Hour

Psalm 143:7—Answer me quickly, O Lord;
my spirit fails.
Do not hide your face from me
or I will be like those who go down
to the pit.

Father in Heaven,

is it all just one big game
of hide and seek?
Are you the tenderhearted *Abba*
whose love causes Him
to dumsily hide half-hidden
so as to be quickly found?
Is your heart's delight
in your children's bounding joy,
as they run to open the door
you have left cracked?
Or do you—as I just might—
take some pleasure in watching us
search in all the wrong places,
before our weariness finally finds you?
O Lord, in this hour I confess,
I've never liked this game
of hide and seek.
I've never understood
why Love would conceal itself,
when a lover only lives
to look on his love's face;
or why divine affection would choose
to withdraw to an unseen place,
when it might be front and center,
tête à tête, hand in hand;
and why life must be filled
with so much weighted wondering,
when a mere glimpse of you, Lord,
might bring the guessing game to an end.
But it seems you've stitched
salvation into the search
and sanctification into the seeking.

233

It appears that to save his life,
   a man must lose himself in searching,
   before he can ever hope to be found.
And no man will find himself,
   until he struggles to find you—
until fumbling with faith,
   he seeks for his lost treasure.
For the Infinite slips through
   the fingers of every greedy grasp,
until by faith, the separation narrows,
   and you, O Lord, draw near
   to the heart drawing near to you.
Hide and seek, seek and find—
      the game of God
   that sets a soul's trajectory.
Whether it is God or man who hides,
   only God knows,
      for it is God's game.
But one thing is clear—
   the soul that does not seek,
      shall never find.
Yet, if a man seeks God from his *there*,
   no matter where his *there* may be,
he will find you, Lord, if he looks for you
   with all his heart and all his soul—
so long as you do the calling,
   and your love loves him first.
For no man's affection will lead him
      to a God in hiding,
   unless the Spirit keeps calling his name.
Face to face, you spoke with men
   from the fire on the mountain;
and though you came out of hiding, Lord,
   your glory and majesty
      did not consume them in flame.
But the mountain is now dark,
   and only an ancient, whispering voice
      rolls down its slopes.
So faith must be the fire of belief,
   burning in the eyes that fail to see;
with courage, it must look beyond the mountain
   to the distant reward still hiding
      from the seeking of earnest eyes.

234

Selected Readings for Further Study

† Deuteronomy 5:1-5; 23-33

† Hebrews 11:1-6

Questions for Reflection and Prayer:

1. Isaiah says to the Lord, "Truly you are a God who hides Himself"(Isa 45:15). What does he mean? Does God hide from man, or does man hide from God (Ge 3:10)? And who does the seeking: God, man, or both?

2. Philosopher Paul Tillich says the following concerning the role of faith:

> He who has faith is separated from the object of his faith. Otherwise he would possess it. It would be a matter of immediate certainty and not of faith....But the human situation, its finitude and estrangement, prevents a man's participation in the ultimate without both the separation and the promise of faith.

As Tillich points out, in a relationship with an invisible, impalpable God, only faith allows the believer to participate with his "ultimate concern." How does faith allow us to "participate" with God? Does faith give us the eyes to see God?

3. In describing his journey to faith, Tolstoy *felt* the tension between the finite and the Infinite. He says, "Resolving the contradiction between finitude and infinity, answering the question of life so as to make life possible, is both necessary and precious." How have you resolved that "contradiction"? Holding on to the faith that follows becomes a lifelong challenge. But as the writer of Hebrews reminds us, it has its rewards (11:6). What are the rewards of faith, present tense and future?

References
Dt 4:29; 5:1-5; 23-33; Pr 2:4-5; 8:17; Isa 45:15; 55:16; Jer 29:13;
Heb 11:1-6; Jas 4:8; 2 Pe 3:18

Diving Deeper:

1. J.D. Eubanks, MD, "From There" in *More of Him, Less of Me* (Dawn Treader, LLC, 2018), 14.
2. Paul Tillich, *Dynamics of Faith* (New York: HarperCollins, 2009), 116.
3. Leo Tolstoy, *A Confession* (Joseph Simon Publisher, 1981), 134.

The Seventy-second Hour

Psalm 143:8a—Let the morning bring me word
of your [the Lord's] unfailing love,
for I have put my trust in you.

O Lord, love without trust

is akin to faith without hope—
    flightless birds of a feather.
For no man loves,
    till he dares to trust;
or clings to faith,
    till he has the courage to hope.
But how thin and tenuous the line
    stretching between our hands—
        that filament of certainty
    on which so much depends!
And the farther you let me run, Lord,
    the stronger I have to pull,
    to keep the tether of this trust taut.
For trust is born of walking together,
    side by side, hand in hand—
proximity proves your Presence,
    as the miles demonstrate consistency,
    the grip confirms compassion,
        and the candid conversation
    communicates your heart's sincerity.
Those who know you best, God,
    have walked with you the longest.
But when you release your hand
    and give us to scattering winds,
can we be confident your love drives us
    to predestined places?
Will the ductility of my trust
    survive this heavenly stretch?
Only you know, Lord,
    for you made the metal I'm made of—
You brought me out of the womb;
    you made me to trust you
    even at my mother's breast.

236

Yet in this hour I confess, God,
  not to questioning your competence,
  but to critiquing your calculus.
For I fear I'm not the man
  you think I am.
And when your storms drive me
  to these barren places,
I'm not sure I have within my pod
    the seed you need
  to plant your Kingdom's tree.
For if those holy brothers broke your trust
  in a moment's frustration,
who am I to manifest your Presence
  when I've hit the rock
  more times than I can count?
But if I don't place my trust in you, O Lord,
    then who?
And if I don't hope in your unfailing love,
  then what hope is there for faith?
For only a blind fool trusts himself;
    and no man's vault of gold is large enough
  to bargain with a hungry grave
    ready to swallow him whole.
In an uncertain world,
  certainty must cling to trust;
and only the one who trusts in you, Lord,
  will not be disappointed.
Though prayers appear unanswered
  and troubles keep mounting,
the one who puts his confidence in Christ
  will be like a tree planted by the water
    that sends out its roots by the stream.
  It does not fear when heat comes;
    its leaves are always green.
  It has no worries in a year of drought
    and never fails to bear fruit.
For when he walked with God,
  he learned His Name—
  "*I AM who I AM.*"
And in His Holy Name, *Yahweh* holds
  both ends of love's fragile line—
    and the one who leans into Love,
  will never be let go.

237

Selected Readings for Further Study

† Jeremiah 17:5-10

† John 8:12-30

Questions for Reflection and Prayer:

1. How are faith and trust different? Can you have faith without trust, or trust without faith? Can trust exist outside of relationship? As it pertains to one's relationship of trust with God, what is one of the primary differences between a new believer and a seasoned believer?

2. In his discussion about "What Faith is Not," philosopher Paul Tillich says:

> Faith is more than trust in authorities, although trust is an element of faith....The Christian may believe in the biblical writers, but not unconditionally. He does not have faith in them. He should not even have faith in the Bible. For faith is more than trust in even the most sacred authority. It is participation in the subject of one's ultimate concern with one's whole being.

What important distinction is Tillich making between faith and trust?

3. Oswald Chambers says, "Watch for the storms of God. The only way God plants His saints is through the whirlwind of His storms. Will you be proven to be an empty pod with no seed inside?" When God brings storms to your life, can you trust He will disperse your life to places where you can grow? What can you do to ensure your life is not an "empty pod with no seed inside"?

References:
   Nu 20:12; Dt 1:32; Ps 9:10; 22:9; 49:13; Pr 3:5; 28:26; Isa 8:17; 30:15;
   Jer 17:5-10; 48:7; Ro 10:11; 1 Pe 2:6

Diving Deeper:

1. J.D. Eubanks, MD, "Live by Faith" in *More of Him, Less of Me* (Dawn Treader, LLC, 2018), 217.
2. Oswald Chambers, *My Utmost for His Highest* (Grand Rapids, MI: Discovery House Publishers, 2012), March 11.
3. Paul Tillich, *Dynamics of Faith* (New York: HarperOne, 2009), 37-38.

The Seventy-third Hour

Psalm 143:8b—Show me the way I should go,
for to you [Lord] I lift up my soul.

The trinity in me, O Lord,
  is body, soul, and spirit—
    three persons within the person.
When you made me in your image, God,
  you cleaved me along Heaven's lines;
for if man must mirror the Master,
  then one must be three,
    and three must be one.
Yet your house is not divided;
  and even when you throne is in Heaven,
    your foot on earth,
  and your Spirit in hearts hiding,
    your three are always in unity.
But my soul is a sojourner,
  a moon pulled by two planets
    into a wobbling orbit.
Sometimes the gravity of the flesh
  tugs the soul away,
until the spirit's orbit comes close enough
  to draw its moon back.

    ~

In this hour I confess, Lord,
  I do not know where to go.
I'm spinning in circles,
  running a race, one revolution at a time,
    never knowing
  if I'm running in vain.
It's too late to go back,
  and too early to call it quits;
and to change courses now,
  would make me a mockery.
Either I've lived a fool's errand
  for a glorious pack of lies,
or your way has a long latency,
  stuck in a seemingly endless Saturday
  between death and resurrection.

But whatever truth proves true,
  I've pitched my tent with you, Lord.
So show me the way; reveal your course.
  Be my Guide under an expansive sky
    filled with stellar signs.
For my soul is here and there,
  essence and sentience,
bound by the body,
  freed by the spirit—
    a wobbling will in constant tension.
The mind is a muddler,
  a mischief maker readily handled
    by the Liar's lilting notes.
But though his legions may kill my body,
  only you, Lord, can destroy my soul.
So come down and lay Heaven's causeway
    through my mapless darkness,
    or I might just spin off course into space.

      ~

I lift my soul up to you, Lord;
  my heart is in my hands.
But my arms are wearied
  by the weight of waiting.
And unless you support
  one limb with Aaron,
    and the other with Hur,
  the battle will soon be lost.
For my soul's weight
  is a heavy world
    my arms can no longer raise.
But to you, God, it's a piffling pennyweight,
  priceless but not ponderous,
and your shoulders are strong enough
  to carry the coinage of us all.
For you are the galaxies' great Galleon,
  who has left His port for a distant shore,
to stock a bottomless haul
  with this world's rare treasures.
No ocean will sink you, Lord;
  no storm will drive us to the depths.
And soon your final Sun will rise
  over the harbor of our hopes.

Selected Readings for Further Study

† Exodus 17:8-16

† 1 Thessalonians 5:16-28

Questions for Reflection and Prayer:

1. What does it mean to "lift up your soul" to the Lord? Is that what Moses was doing before the Lord during the battle with the Amalekites? How about when Hannah "poured out her soul" before the Lord (1 Sam 1:15)?

2. In 1907, Dr. Duncan MacDougall published the findings of his experiments—in which he sought to define the weight of the soul—on six dying patients. After meticulous measurements (which he later compared to similar experiments on dogs), MacDougall concluded that the human soul weighs 21 grams: a mere pocket full of pennies. However, as many of us know, sometimes the soul's weight may feel insufferably heavy—like a ton of bricks. When the soul feels weighed down, what does the Psalmist encourage us to do (Ps 42:5-6; 43:5)?

3. In his letter to the Galatians, the Apostle Paul admits to a fear that he was "running or had run his race in vain" (2:2). Have you ever felt that way? Have you ever questioned whether all that you have lived for is really real? Can Paul's momentary weakness of faith be an encouragement to you today?

References:
        Ex 17:8-16; 1 Sam 1:15; Ps 42:5-6; 43:5; Gal 2:2; 1 Thes 5:23-24

Diving Deeper:

1. J.D. Eubanks, MD, "Running in Vain?" in *More of Him, Less of Me* (Dawn Treader, LLC, 2018), 318.
2. Billy Graham, "The Value of Your Soul," *Decision Magazine* (July 28, 2012), https://decisionmagazine.com/value-your-soul/ (accessed April 11, 2023).
3. Ben Thomas, "The man who tried to weigh the soul," *Discover Magazine*, (Nov 3, 2015), https://www.discovermagazine.com/mind/the-man-who-tried-to-weigh-the-soul (accessed April 14, 2023).

Psalm 143:9—Rescue me from my enemies, O Lord;
for I hide myself in you.

To hide in you, O God,

I must abide in you;
to be rescued from my enemies,
  I must live within your walls.
For you are the great City on the hill;
  and the refuge you promise the running
    dwells inside your gates.
Will I enter your rest?
  Will I choose to remain in your domain?
Many forces pursue me;
  their ranks spread out
    like sand on the shore.
But the enemy I fear most
  is the one I cannot see;
and the hound I cannot shake,
  is the one who knows my smell too well.
For the man in me is my nemesis;
  without fail he finds me out.
And if I hide myself in you, Lord,
  will you hide me from myself?
He who dwells in the shelter of the Most High
  will rest in the shadow of the Almighty.
But will your shadow overshadow mine?
  And though the wings of your Presence
    may shelter me from ten thousand,
  will they deliver me from the only one
    whose pursuit refuses to relent?
I need a Savior who saves me from me;
  I need a Refuge who rescues
    a sinner deep-set.
Your Name, O Lord, is a strong tower,
  and the righteous who run to you
    find the safety they desire.

But no one is righteous until you right them;
   and no righteousness redeems,
   until you, God, release the regenerate.
So to hide in you, Lord,
   you must abide in me,
      till I remain in you—
   hidden with Christ in God;
dead but alive, alive but somehow dead,
   concealed until you appear.
For a branch without the vine
   is fit for the fire;
a life without your Life, Lord,
   is a bramble set for burning.
But with Love inside,
   the fruit tastes sweet,
and even the briar patch
   blooms into berries
   to feed the hungry heart.
For when your love chooses to remain, Lord,
   the branches never wither
   and the fruit lasts forever.
"Because he loves me," says the Lord,
      "I will rescue him;
   I will protect him, for he acknowledges
      my Name.
He will call upon me, and I will answer him;
   I will be with him in trouble,
   I will deliver him and honor him.
With long life will I satisfy him
   and show him my salvation."
Your love, O Lord,
   is my new lease on life.
So when the life I once lived
   comes knocking at my door;
when trouble tracks me down,
   and my dying man
      reaches for me to drown;
claim my tenancy in you, Lord,
   and rescue this refugee,
      whose hiding is joyful abiding.

Selected Readings for Further Study

† Psalm 91

† Colossians 3:1-11

Questions for Reflection and Prayer:

1. Walt Kelly—author of the comic strip *Pogo*—says in his 1970 Earth Day comic strip, "We have met the enemy and he is us." How can we become our own worst enemy? Who is your biggest enemy? Is it, perhaps, you?

2. In his book on courage, *New York Times* best-selling author, Ryan Holiday, says:

> No amount of hiding will actually protect you from scary things. We are already fugitives from the law of averages, we are already marked for death from birth....All certainty is uncertainty. You're not safe. You never will be. No one is.

From a human perspective, Holiday is quite right to say, "All certainty is uncertainty." But as Oswald Chambers reminds us, "gracious uncertainty is the mark of the spiritual life." We can hide ourselves in God and be certain His faithfulness will guard, protect, and keep us safe amidst the "uncertainties" of life (Pr 29:25; Ps 32:7; 138:7; 2 Thes 3:3). Are you hiding in God?

3. What does it mean to abide in the Lord (Jn 15:5-10)? Andrew Murray says, "Abiding in Jesus is nothing but the giving up of oneself to be ruled and taught and led, and so resting in the arms of Everlasting Love." Are you abiding in God?

References
      Isa 25:4; 26:1-5; Ps 27:5; 31:19-20; 32:7; 64:2; 68:20; 91; Pr 18:10; 29:20; Jn 15:5-10; Ro 3:10; 2 Cor 5:17; Eph 3:17-19; Col 3:3

Diving Deeper:

1. J.D. Eubanks, MD, "Remain" in *More of Him, Less of Me* (Dawn Treader, LLC, 2018), 37.
2. Ryan Holiday, *Courage is Calling* (New York: Penguin, 2021), 62-63.
3. Oswald Chambers, *My Utmost For His Highest* (Grand Rapids, MI: Discovery House Publishers, 1992), April 29.
3. Andrew Murray, *Abide in Christ* in *Collected Works on Prayer* (New Kensington: Whitaker House, 2013), 25.

The Seventy-fifth Hour

> Psalm 143:10—Teach me to do your [the Lord's] will,
> for you are my God;
> may your good Spirit
> lead me on level ground.

H eavenly Father, your way
　is a rough and rocky road,
　　lined by dissenters, littered with tripping stones—
an upward march to Golgotha.
My Lord said to my Lord,
　"*You are my Son,
　　today I have become your Father.*"
And yet, even the Son stumbled His cross
　up the mountain's nape,
　　to the bald head's brutality.
He learned obedience from what He suffered;
　until the spear pierced His side,
　　He was a student of God's will.
God learned from God,
　so men might learn
　　from the lashings of Love.
The lily of the field
　and the birds of the air
　　seem to know it best:
　　there are no half-measures.
With petals unfurled, wings spread out,
　they declare the divine, "Either/or!"
*Either love God or—hate him,
　either hold fast to him or—despise him.*[17]
Be dressed in the Kingdom's robes,
　and ride on a wimpling wing;
drink what Heaven drops,
　and eat what her earth delivers.
Be unconditionally in the will
　for which you were made, or—

---

[17] Søren Kierkegaard, *The Lily of the Field and the Bird of the Air* (Princeton, NJ: Princeton University Press, 2016), 44.

245

everything else is an indifference,
  a vanishing vapor passing under the sun—
    here today, gone tomorrow.
Creation is your classroom, Lord,
  and your good Spirit
  guides the guilty by the guiltless.
Learn from the lily and the bird:
  silence, obedience, and joy—
    "Not my will, but yours be done."
Carry out unconditionally
  the conditions of today—
  morning's chorus, midday's aerie-adding,
    and evening's feasting.
Submit unreservedly
  to push up into the unrelenting sun,
to stand on a flimsy stalk
  before wind, rain, and swelter.
Be simple enough to simply believe,
  everything that happens
  is unconditionally God's will.
For even chance bows to providence,
  and science genuflects before sovereignty.
And if the universe obeys,
  who am I to resist?
If God submits to God,
  by what delusion may I defy Divinity?
But willing your will, O Lord,
  is still a rough and rocky road
  you call us to smooth through you.
For a voice cries out in the desert,
  in cactus blooms and buntings,
"Prepare the way for the Lord,
make straight paths for Him.
Every valley shall be filled in,
every mountain and hill made low.
The crooked shall be made straight,
and the rough ways smooth.
And all mankind will see God's salvation."
Creation cries out, "What will you do?"
  The sparrow's song and the lily's dance
    declare, "I will will His will!"—
    Will you?

Selected Readings for Further Study

† Isaiah 40:1-8

† Hebrews 5:1-10

Questions for Reflection and Prayer:

1. In reflecting upon Hebrews 5, Andrew Murray reminds us:

> Christ needed suffering that in it He might learn to obey and give up His will to the Father at any cost....He learned obedience, He became obedient unto death, that He might become the author of our salvation. He became the author of our salvation through obedience, that He might save those "who obey Him."

Christ deigned to learn obedience to the Father's will so that we might be saved. In His suffering, He also taught us how to obey. Are you learning obedience in your suffering?

2. Kierkegaard says, "For in nature everything is nothing, understood in the sense that there is nothing other than God's unconditional will; at the same instant that it is not unconditionally God's will, it has ceased to exist." For Kierkegaard, life itself exists within God's will. Either you're in His will, or you cease to exist. Are you in God's will?

3. The writer of Hebrews recounts that when Christ came into the world He said, "Here I am—it is written about me in the scroll—I have come to do your will, O God" (10:7). Is your name also written on God's scroll (Mal 3:16)? Have you, like Christ, come to do God's will or your own?

References
    Isa 40:1-8; Mal 3:16; Mt 6:25-34; Lk 4:18-19; Heb 5:1-10; 10:7

Diving Deeper:

1. J.D. Eubanks, MD, "I Will" in *More of Him, Less of Me* (Dawn Treader, LLC, 2018), 67.
2. Søren Kierkegaard, *The Lily of the Field and the Bird of the Air* (Princeton, NJ: Princeton University Press, 2016), 49-50.
3. Andrew Murray, *The School of Obedience* (Public Domain).

The Seventy-sixth Hour

Psalm 143:11—For your name's sake, O Lord, preserve my life;
in your righteousness, bring me out of trouble.

W hat's in a name, O Lord?

For surely that which we call a rose
by any other name
would smell just as sweet.[18]
And yet your Name, *Yahweh,*
is Alpha and Omega,
and no whimsical mistake.
It is the primeval atom,
from which all other atoms come—
the universe bound up
in six infinite letters.
A man may change his name
and find his destiny follows:
For you made Abram, Abraham,
to father your promise;
you dubbed Jacob, Israel,
to build your nation;
Saul was transformed into Paul,
to reach the world's corners;
and you claimed Simon as Peter,
to hold the keys of your Church.
A name may hold our fate,
but fate falls
before your Almighty Name.
For while we may change,
your Name remains the same.
And before your Name, Lord,
every knee will bow,
in Heaven and on earth and under earth,
and every tongue confess
that Jesus Christ is Lord,
to the glory of God the Father.
So in this hour I pray, O Lord,
for the sake of your Name,

---

[18] William Shakespeare, *Romeo and Juliet*, Act 2, sc. 1, l.85-86.

248

preserve my weary spirit.
See the emblem of your love in me,
   a banner bearing your Name
     in a costly war.
And because you have exalted
   your Name and word above all things,
send me the strong arms I need
   to keep your standard standing.
For the ensign I bear
   is shot through and leaning,
and the hillock I hold,
   besieged on every side.
And if you do not come quickly,
   every inch of ground
     your great Name has claimed in me,
   might soon be lost.
For surely it was for your name's sake
   you have forgiven my sins;
now may the glory of your Name
   deliver me in this hour.
For the sake of your great Name,
   guide me in paths of righteousness.
Open a road in the bottom of the sea;
   drive the depths into rising walls
   that declare your mighty power.
Save me from the doubt
   that threatens to drown me;
rescue me from my chasing chariots,
   and cover them in a watery grave.
But you, O Sovereign Lord,
   deal well with me for your name's sake;
   out of the goodness of your love, deliver me.
Then I will walk with you, Lord,
   through a world of false gods,
to declare before the altar of the Unknown
   the Name that is above every name.
And when the crowd queries,
   "What's in a Name?"
I shall in like respond,
   "What's not?"
For in Him we live and move
   and have our being.

Selected Readings for Further Study

† Genesis 17:5-9; 32:22-32

† Acts 17:16-34

Questions for Reflection and Prayer:

1. Shakespeare's love-struck Juliet famously asks, "What's in a name? That which we call a rose/ By any other word would smell as sweet." Maybe, as Juliet suggests, names are arbitrary and meaningless. But as Salman Rushdie reminds us, in the East names carry a much different weight: "Our names contain our fates; living as we do in a place where names have not acquired the meaninglessness of the West, and are still more than mere sounds, we are also the victims of our titles." What is the biblical understanding of a name's worth? How does God value His name? Is God a "victim" of His name, or does He reign in His name?

2. The third commandment reminds us God's name is holy. Indeed, it is synonymous with "holiness" and "glory." All that God does in our lives and the world at large, He does for His name's sake. When we misuse His name, we sin. Have you been careful with God's name?

3. When the Apostle Paul stands before the meeting of the Areopagus, he puts a Name on the altar "TO AN UNKNOWN GOD." Have you been this bold in your life. Are you declaring the Name of God to a world that has marginalized it or forgotten it?

References
Ge 17:5-9; 32:28; Ps 23:3; 79:9; 106:8; 109:21; 138:2 138:2; Mal 3:6; Jn 1:42; Acts 13:9; Php 2:9-11

Diving Deeper:

1. J.D. Eubanks, MD, "Finding Truth" in *More of Him, Less of Me* (Dawn Treader, LLC, 2018), 201.
2. Justin Taylor, "For the Sake of God's Name," (January 5, 2012), https://www.thegospelcoalitioorg/blogs/justin-taylor/for-the-sake-of-gods-name/, (accessed April 29, 2023).
3. William Shakespeare, *Romeo and Juliet*, Act 2, sc. 1, l.85-86.
4. Salman Rushdie, *Midnight's Children* (New York: Alfred A. Knopf, 1995), 386.

The Seventy-seventh Hour

Psalm 143:12—In your [the Lord's] unfailing love, silence my enemies;
destroy all my foes,
for I am your servant.

Y ou have called me, O Lord,

to be a servant of the Servant,
who came not to be served, but to serve.
You have asked me to do as you have done—
to bow at the feet of the broken,
and wash the weary soles
in your Spirit's bottomless basin.
Unfailing Love has an infinite reach;
it blows through walls,
slips through the cracks,
fills every gap
and passes through.
Even the untouchable can be touched;
even the pariah can be embraced.
But my love is full of my failings,
and my reach restricted
by a leaden reason.
Where there are prophecies, they will cease;
where there are tongues, they will be stilled;
where there is knowledge, it will pass away.
For we know in part and we prophesy in part,
but when perfection comes,
the imperfect disappears—
Love never fails, though I often do;
and though I see but a poor reflection
as in a clouded mirror,
one day I will see clearly,
face to face.
But until *vis à vis*, your face, O Lord, hides
in furrowed brows and downcast eyes.
It lives in tear-drenched cheeks;
it is behind every downtrodden frown.
And to leave my childhood behind,
I must tenderly behold
the vexed visage of God.

251

But who can stare into this sorrow
  without sinking?
Who can shoulder this cross
  without falling?
For only God can peer into our depths
    and emerge to serve
  the brokenness He has observed.
Only the Lord can feed His enemy;
    only Heaven can heap burning coals on his head
    with a cup of cold water.
Only Jehovah can give His staff
  to the one who has stolen His cloak;
and only Jesus can turn the other cheek
  to the one who has struck Him.
Serve as you have served, Lord,
  what man can do it?
Unless, you do the doing;
    unless, the Spirit climbs inside
    to reclaim the unfaithful bride.
More of Him, less of me,
  the servant serves best
    who finds himself the least.
The lover loves most true,
  when he loses himself to Love.
And he who would be the greatest,
  must deign to become the least.
For the one who wishes to be filled,
  must consent to be emptied
    by Love, for love's sake.
The servant is a mural of stained glass
  Heaven's essence washes through.
And the story of grace, power, and love
    his life is meant to tell,
  is best told when the Light
    filters through his paneled soul.
Then the Sun's rays
  will be high and lifted up,
as they tell of a God who came down
  to make Himself nothing,
    taking the very nature of a servant,
  so a sleeping Church might rise
    rejoicing into the Light.
O Lord, awaken my night!

Selected Readings for Further Study

† Psalm 57:8-11

† 1 Corinthians 13:8-13

Questions for Reflection and Prayer:

1. C.S. Lewis says, "Our whole destiny seems to lie…in being as little as possible ourselves…[and] becoming clean mirrors filled with the image of a face that is not ours." Abraham Heschel goes on to say: "faith only comes when we stand face to face—the ineffable in us with the ineffable beyond us…." When your faith finally allows you to "see clearly," whose face will you see in the mirror? Yours or Christ's?

2. In her poem, "The Blessing of the Old Woman, the Tulip, and the Dog," poet Alicia Suskin Ostriker writes, "To be blessed/…is to live and work/ so hard/ God's love/ washes right through you…." Have you learned the blessing of the servant: allowing God's love to "wash right through you"?

3. The Apostle Paul tells the Colossians, "I fill up in my flesh what is still lacking in regard to Christ's afflictions….(Col 1:24-25). How can Christ's afflictions be lacking? What does Paul mean? Does the suffering Paul alludes to refer to his role as a servant of Christ's Church? Are you a fellow servant in this suffering?

References
> Ps 57: 4-11; Mt 5:38-42; 23:11; Lk 22:24-27; Ro 12:20; 1 Cor 13:8-12
> Php 2:7; Col 1:24-25

Diving Deeper:

1. J.D. Eubanks, MD, "He Must Increase, I Must Decrease" in *More of Him, Less of Me* (Dawn Treader, LLC, 2018), 22.
2. C.S. Lewis, *The Business of Heaven* (New York: HarperCollins, 1984), 267.
3. Abraham Joshua Heschel, *Man is Not Alone* (New York: Farrar, Straus, and Giroux, 1951), 91.
4. Alicia Suskin Ostriker, "The Blessing of the Old Woman, the Tulip, and the Dog," https://www.poetryfoundation.org/poems/53677/the-blessing-of-the-old-woman-the-tulip-and-the-dog (accessed 5/7/2023).
5. Phil Thompson, "What does it mean to 'Fill up what's lacking in Christ's afflictions'?" October 11, 2020,
https://www.thegospelcoalition.org/article/lacking-in-christs-afflictions/ (accessed 5/7/2023).

Acknowledgements

I am so very thankful for all those friends and family members whose prayers and support have helped sustain me throughout the composition of this book. For the time in which this project was written was unquestionably one of the most difficult periods of my life. Not unlike C.S. Lewis—who struggled to jump inside the demonic mind to write *The Screwtape Letters*—I struggled to jump inside my own beleaguered mind during the creative process transpiring in this difficult time. But through providential grace and the faithful prayers of God's people (2 Cor 1:10-11), *Book of Hours* has emerged from this arduous journey. I comfort in this truth: there is no art, much less heart refinement, without suffering.

255

ABOUT THE AUTHOR

Dr. Eubanks is blessed to be a pilgrim making progress on his journey home. On the way, his mission field is currently medicine, where he serves an Associate Professor of Orthopaedic Surgery at Case Western Reserve University School of Medicine and the Chief and Director of Spine Surgery at University Hospitals Ahuja Medical Center. He is the author of *Twelve Stones: Apologetics for an Age of Relativism, Gentlest of Ways, More of Him, Less of Me: A Doctor's Devotional for Spiritual Health, For the Joy of Obeying,* and a volume of poetry entitled, *Rotations: A Medical Student's Clinical Experience.* He has written over 20 peer-reviewed scientific publications, multiple textbook chapters and editorials, and poetry appearing in journals such as *JAMA, The Annals of Internal Medicine, Tar River Poetry,* and more. He lives outside of Cleveland, Ohio.

www.ingramcontent.com/pod-product-compliance
Lightning Source LLC
Chambersburg PA
CBHW072340090426
42741CB00012B/2857